CONTENTS

1. "I Can't Imagine Myself Witnessing" 7
2. People Who Should Not Witness 13
3. Some People Who Discovered It Could Be Done 21
4. "How Do I Begin?" 36
5. "How Do I Present the Gospel?" 44
6. Have a Gentle Attitude 53
7. Don't Be Afraid 61
8. Reverse Psychology and Auto-Suggestion 70
9. People Who Find Fault With God 76
10. Witness During the Crises of Life 92
11. Learn to Close 105
12. Perpetuate the Gospel 112

Too Good to Keep!

Jess Moody

While this book is designed for the reader's personal enjoyment, it is also intended for group study. A Leader's Guide with Victor Multiuse Transparency Masters is available from your local bookstore or from the publisher.

VICTOR BOOKS
a division of SP Publications, Inc.
WHEATON, ILLINOIS 60187

Offices also in Fullerton, California • Whitby, Ontario, Canada • Amersham-on-the-Hill, Bucks, England

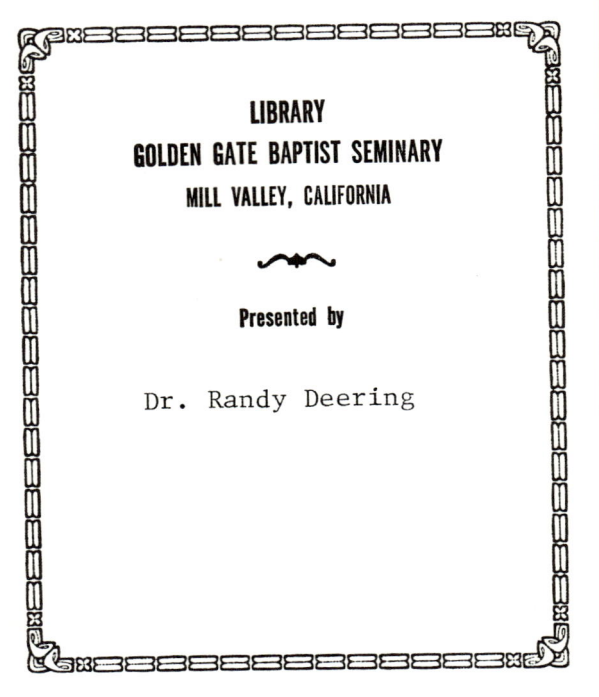

of the Bible.

Recommended Dewey Decimal Classification: 253.4
  Suggested Subject Heading: WITNESSING

Library of Congress Catalog Card Number: 81-52895
ISBN: 0-89693-006-8

© 1982 by SP Publications, Inc. All rights reserved
Printed in the United States of America

VICTOR BOOKS
A division of SP Publications, Inc.
P.O. Box 1825 ● Wheaton, Illinois 60187

To
Franklin Morgan

"One man plus God is the answer."

ONE
"I Can't Imagine Myself Witnessing"

She was a beautiful woman, an avid reader, a glib conversationalist, but a rather lukewarm Christian who could take her church or leave it. Her face had registered total disbelief as she listened to my message, "Anyone Can Be a Witness." When the service was over, she asked if we could talk.

As we sat on the front pew of the church, her initial words were both a statement and a question: "You can't have been serious! You don't understand human nature. The only people who 'witness' are red-necked Bible-bangers or misfits seeking recognition." She was not belligerent, but was expressing an honest viewpoint from her frame of reference.

"If you truly believe what you just said," I answered, "why did you bother to talk to me?"

She replied, "Your message indicated that even a casual, reasonably well-educated, moderately sophisticated, somewhat liberated woman should be able to share her faith with others, and I just wanted to investigate further. I haven't heard other educated people make the kind of statements you made."

"That indicates," I said, "that either I am not very well educated or that your arena of experience has not yet included what I know to be a veritable army of normal people who have a faith to share and want to share it, in order to help fellow human beings whom they love."

I told her that any Christian anywhere is a witness of some kind, that witnessing is a gift given to all believing children of God, and that all Christians are commanded to witness. No Christian is shut off from the beautiful opportunity of sharing his faith, however insecure he may feel or limited his talent may be.

I then showed her some Bible passages which would indicate where I was coming from:

- Acts 18:24-28, the story of Aquila and Priscilla, two loving Christians who were simple witnesses.
- Acts 8, Philip the evangelist witnessing to the Ethiopian
- Acts 20:20-21, which tells of Paul's zeal in witnessing
- 2 Timothy 1:5 and 3:15, parents witnessing to their children
- John 1, where a teacher led his pupils to Christ, a brother shared his faith with his brother, and a friend communicated the Gospel to a friend (vv. 29, 40-41, 45).

I asked her if she believed in Satan. With a wisp of despair in her voice, and reflecting more than she intended of her background, she said, "Oh, yes. Sometimes I believe more in the reality of Satan than I do of God."

I asked her, "If you were Satan, how would you go about paralyzing the Christian movement?"

"By eliminating its most effective weapon."

"Exactly. Any enemy is defeated by weakening his firepower."

"You speak as though we are in a war," she said.

"We *are* in a war. 'We wrestle not against flesh and blood, but against principalities and powers,' (Eph. 6:12). The Christian's chief weapon for changing the world is his sharing of a personal experience with Jesus Christ. If I were Satan I would weaken, belittle, and reduce to the absurd this one weapon which every Christian has as a gift from God."

This lovely lady could not imagine herself witnessing! Perhaps you have the same problem. As I challenged her, so I challenge you to utilize your chief weapon for helping Christ's revolution change the world: personal evangelism. Everyone deserves to be witnessed to. No one should be beyond the reach of hearing about Christ.

There are many things that pull people apart, but the Christian has one covenant with all mankind: the binding covenant to share his faith. It is an amazing proof of Satan's work that we can talk with total freedom about new cars, going shopping, or the weather. But once we begin to speak of Christ, a certain tension enters the situation and tends to neutralize, or emotionalize the conversation.

Who injects this negative tension into the atmosphere? It is Satan. He fosters the belief that witnessing is for a unique kind of person.

"It takes a special kind of animal to be a witness," said my churched friend.

"No," I replied, "there are only two requirements: being human, and having something to witness about. You have these already. If you will supply the willingness, God will cause your witnessing power to grow."

You Can Witness Anywhere
In His humanity, Jesus not only taught us of truth but set the example for witnessing wherever He went. He witnessed in a boat and on the seaside. He witnessed in the temple and in homes.
- Witnessing can be done anywhere.

I have witnessed on an airplane, in an elevator
while traveling aboard ship across the North Sea
in bars, in jails, at a NATO meeting
at a Communist rally in Paris, on a London subway
beside an outhouse, in front of a whorehouse
on a movie set, in a restaurant, in a garden
at a space launch, in a classroom, in a taxicab
at funerals, weddings, baptisms, at a Bar Mitzvah
on a bus, in a car, under a car, on a sailboat
at an engagement party, on the telephone
during a suicide attempt (he succeeded)
on Sunset Boulevard in front of Sneaky Pete's
waiting to see the Passion Play in Oberammergau
in the Russian exhibit in Tokyo, in the Oval Office
in an Israeli government office, in an Arab market
in a Norwegian snowstrom, on a train in Ireland
at a zoo, at Disney World, in a wax museum
in a cotton field, at a hurricane party
at a scientific experiment in Seattle
in an all-night cafe in Skagway, Alaska
on a golf course in Puerto Rico
at a banquet honoring Hank Aaron
in a ghost town in Colorado, in a tree house
at a rodeo, at a pheasant hunt in Kansas
at a stabbing, during a tonsillectomy
at an inauguration of the president of the Senate
at a McDonald's counter, in a planetarium
at a deer hunt, and in a mortuary.
- Witnessing can be done by anybody:

by an auto salesman with a handlebar mustache
an airline pilot, a stewardess, a truck driver
an engineer at a television station
a violinist on the Lawrence Welk Show
a garbage collector, a tire repairman, a philatelist
a numismatist, a mayor's secretary
even a casual churchwoman, if she wants to.

● And witnessing can be done to anyone.
Jesus witnessed to Satan, to two fishermen
to an army captain, to demon-possessed people
to the disciples of John the Baptist, to a leper
to a father whose daughter had just died
to a woman in need of a hysterectomy
to the twelve disciples, to strict Sabbath observers
to a blind man, to farmers, to a prostitute
to a mother with a demon-possessed daughter
to temple tax collectors, to a small child
to the high priest, to a dying thief
to a man He raised from the dead.

The Privilege Is Yours

There is no place where you cannot witness. There is no time when you cannot witness. There is no person to whom you cannot witness. There is no Christian who cannot witness.

Christ said, "Ye shall be witnesses unto Me.... Go ye into all the world, and preach the Gospel to every creature" (Acts 1:8; Mark 16:15).

God never commands us to do that which we cannot do; therefore, with the imperative in the Great Commission (Matthew 28:19-20, Mark 16:15 and Luke 24:46-48), and without specification as to who should be a witness, the logical conclusion is that God commands every Christian everywhere to witness for Christ. *Since He commands it, we can do it.*

Satan would love to cause you to believe that witnessing is a gift like preaching, singing, or teaching—a select gift for only a few. This is a patent falsehood, and it must be repudiated forcefully or the church will die.

If every Christian will stop determining for himself what he wants and instead do what Christ said to do, the Gospel can spread around the world rapidly. Reaching the world for Jesus Christ is not that difficult a task. The only requirement is that every Christian make up his mind. If he is to receive the benefits of prayer and the blessing of God, he must accept the responsibility to witness and the opportunity to see others give themselves to the Lord Jesus Christ.

My friend on the front pew of the church could not imagine that she could ever witness for Christ. But God has made it possible for people, who never dreamed they could be used, to enter into direct dialogue with others about Christ. Every Christian reading this book can go out and witness for the glory of the Lord. What a blessed privilege you have to witness for Him!

TWO
People Who Should Not Witness

The Carnal Christian does not enjoy witnessing. The Carnal Christian will do absolutely anything, short of going to the foreign mission field, to keep from witnessing. He will serve as a deacon, he will serve as a member of the finance committee, he will serve as a Sunday School teacher, as a counter, as an usher, as anything. He does not want to win lost souls to Jesus Christ.

The major problem in the Christian world is the Carnal Christian. He destroys churches and crucifies pastors. He talks spiritually, but inwardly is full of resentment, hatred, self-righteousness, self-justification, and self-motivation. Christ has very little to do with the direction in which his life flows. The Carnal Christian is the enemy of church fellowship and harmony.

The Carnal Christian is a greater problem than communism or universalism. He is in the way. He is THE stumbling block.

Carnality in the Christian does not refer to fleshly, sexual sins. It refers to the dominance of the self, the dominance of the flesh, the dominance of the devi over the Christian's will and therefore over his lifestyle. The Carnal Christian does not usually realize that he is carnal. He does not understand that there is more to the Christian life than he has been experiencing.

It took an in-depth study of the Word of God before I came to understand that Carnal Christians have the same dealings with the Holy Spirit that all believing Christians do. For instance, all believers—including Carnal Christians—are indwelt by the Holy Spirit. I won't go into the details of it, but you may want to read 1 Corinthians 3:16; 6:19; 1 Corinthians 5:5 and 1 Corinthians 6; John 7:37, 39; Acts 11:17; Romans 5:5; 1 Corinthians 2:12; 2 Corinthians 5:5.

Also, all believers are baptized by the Holy Spirit, and this is the most confusing part of the entire doctrine of the Holy Spirit. Many will try to separate conversion from baptism, but it is not possible. You might read Acts 1:5; 2:4-31; 10:44-48; 11:15-17; 1 Corinthians 12:13; Ephesians 4:5; 5:18.

In addition to being indwelt by the Holy Spirit and baptized by the Holy Spirit, the Carnal Christian is sealed by the Holy Spirit (2 Corinthians 1:22; Ephesians 1:13; 4:30).

A Carnal Christian is regenerated, baptized, indwelt, and sealed by the Holy Spirit whether he understands it or not. But one thing is lacking—he is not filled with the Holy Spirit. Ephesians 5:18 refers to a specific command—"Be filled with the Spirit." It is written in the imperative. Acts 2:4 speaks of the Apostles being filled on the Day of Pentecost. The same group was filled a short time after that (Acts 4:31). This filling can be repeated again and again. And the human ego constantly fights against it.

People Who Should Not Witness / 15

I estimate that 90 percent of all non-Christians are unsaved simply because they have not been asked or confronted with the claims of the Gospel. They have no excuses, no defense mechanisms. Most unsaved people are just waiting for some tactful, kind, intelligent, friendly human being to come to them and share the Gospel. Nearly every time that unsaved person will accept Jesus Christ as Saviour. The problem is not with the harvest, but with the harvesters.

The reason 90 percent of the unsaved are still lost is that so many Christians who are regenerated, baptized, indwelt, and sealed by the Holy Spirit have not been filled with the Holy Spirit. They have all the things the Holy Spirit can do *for* a Christian, but have not had that which the Holy Spirit can do *through* Christians to flow from their lives. When a Christian accepts the fullness of the Spirit, he is then set apart and can and will do the good work of witnessing by overflowing.

The church has been crippled through the centuries by soul-winning programs designed to herd unwilling, grumbling Christians into a witnessing format. It is my conviction that *witnessing should not be done by Carnal Christians. Carnal Christians should never be allowed to witness because the work they do is incomplete, spurious, injurious, and stifling.* I have seen so much spiritual fruit that was bruised by the grubby hands of Carnal Christians.

At some time in my future ministry I propose to write a book entitled, *The One and Only Problem of the Church—The Carnal Christian.* The unsaved man is not the main problem, and the Spirit-filled Christian is not a problem. The Carnal Christian is the church's greatest problem. And the great programs designed to "con" the Carnal Christian into the witnessing corral have resulted in one failure after another.

A pastor should lead his people on the journey into the Spirit-filled life, and direct his church in determining who the Spirit-filled people are. Right at this point there is a very great danger, but the danger should not cause the pastor to refrain from this necessary judgment. Those who are not truly Spirit-filled, will probably become smug and pharisaical. But truly Spirit-filled Christians will not have this problem. They will love, for the fruit of the Spirit is love. They will love all the members of the church, and think nothing of the determination about who is Spirit-filled.

The Carnal Christians will make much of it. They will raise unshirted havoc throughout the church family, trying to stop the movement to find the Spirit-filled people in your church family or to urge people to be Spirit-filled. They should be dealt with by ignoring them.

If they become too troublesome, they need strict discipline. The church is very weak on the point of discipline; therefore, it is very weak in discipleship. For there is a direct correlation between discipleship and discipline. If Christians think that the church is a big tantrum arena where they can do anything, say anything, be anything they want to be, and cause any problem in the church they want to cause—and never be corrected for it—they will do exactly that. They must be disciplined. The Carnal Christian will constantly cause trouble unless he is broken and then filled with the Spirit.

I know of several churches whose pastors had to leave, because Carnal Christians dominated the board, the finance committee, and the Sunday School. No pastor can work with uncooperative, fault-finding, self-righteous egomaniacs. So the pastor leaves and the carnality goes on from one generation to the next. This is a disgrace in the sight of God, a stench in His nostrils, and the real reason judgment is brewing for the American church.

At the First Baptist Church of Van Nuys, one Sunday morning we conducted two services which we entitled, "The Roar of Revolution." This involved the use of the booklet *"Have You Experienced the Spirit-Filled Life?"* published by Campus Crusade. Every member of the congregation was given a copy and asked to choose a partner with whom to read the book aloud.

It was a roar of revolution indeed. At the end of the hour, they were challenged to claim the Spirit-filled life. I asked them to bow their heads in silence. Gradually the roar abated into silence, and there came a holy hush in the sanctuary. Many lives were transformed that day. The mail the following week was tremendous. People had problems solved in family relationships, attitudes, stewardship, and in service. The deepening in the church life was greatly needed and long overdue. A new love permeated the family. The Carnal Christians began to react violently, doing everything they could to avoid submission to the Spirit and to the body of Christ, but they did not prevail.

As we think of how to get a church to respond to a true soul-winning challenge, we need to remember that 90 percent of all the unsaved are unsaved simply because the church doesn't go to them, not because they have hang-ups, questions, or problems. They are waiting; they know not what for, but actually they are waiting for you. A Spirit-filled body of Jesus Christ is the sweetest thing this side of heaven. A carnal church represents other geography.

Repentance

There are all kinds of soul-winning techniques, but none of them will do any good if you refuse to witness. If you are still in a state of sinful rebellion against God's command to go, and have not yet settled the issue of your willingness to go, all the techniques are valueless. In fact, for you to learn one new soul-winning technique will make you more guilty than if you did not learn it—if you do not intend to win people to Jesus Christ. Don't learn anything else from God's Book. Don't study another verse of Scripture. Stay away from the Bible unless you're going to do what it says. If the Lord tells you in His Word to do something, it must be done or you're living in disobedience.

So right now I want you to put this book down, bow your head and confess to God what a wicked, sinful Christian you've been because you've refused to go out and win souls to Christ. All these years you've been enjoying the privileges and the joys of His blessings, but have not taken the responsibility that He has asked you to take.

Pray a prayer something like this: "Dear God, I'm a wicked sinner. I have presumed upon Your grace and mercy to a horrible degree. I confess the intense evil of the sin of silence, and I ask You to make my lips instruments to communicate the lovely truth of Jesus Christ, the Saviour of men. I surrender my life to You. May the Holy Spirit give me the motivation and courage to do the will of God. In Jesus' name, Amen."

Then get up from your knees, pick up this book, and continue in the study. But don't wait until you finish reading to start witnessing. Is there someone in the next room right now who does not know the Saviour? Go and talk with him about it. Is there someone who comes to your mind at this moment? Call him and make an appointment to see him today. And remember, your purpose is to share what Christ has done for you. You must put the *now* into the commandments of Christ, or the commandments of Christ will become instruments of awful judgment against you. "Therefore, to him that knoweth to do good, and doeth it not, to him it is sin" (James 4:17).

Imagizing

One of the first things that motivated me to start winning people to Jesus Christ was the power of imagining and visualizing, which I call imagizing. I want you to imagize some friend of yours who is not a Christian. I want you to see him or her vitally involved in the service of the Lord. Then I want you to see that person in hell forever without God and without hope, simply because you didn't go and tell him. I want you to visualize the pain, the agony, the loneliness, the despair, the unfulfillment, the godless reprobation, the fowl breath of hate in the pit of hell. Imagine it. Feel for your friend the pain he is going to go through—the pain, the sorrow, the darkness, the despair.

Then do what I said originally. Imagize him saved. I want you to see him or her being baptized by your pastor into the church. I want you to see the church members gathering around him, congratulating him, telling him how proud and happy they are that he has received Jesus Christ as his Saviour. I want you to see him getting over his depression, his loneliness, despair, or hate. I want you to see him with a smile on his face and feel the joy in his heart—all because you told him about Jesus.

THREE
Some People Who Discovered It Could Be Done

When I was a sophomore at Baylor University, my interest in spiritual things was not as deep as it should have been. I was mildly interested in academics, and wildly interested in athletics and girls. It had been a desire of mine for quite some time to be an effective communicator. I reasoned that no matter what position I held in the future, I would have to relate to people and communicate the ideas from my brain to their brains. With that in mind, I decided to take an elective course in journalism. I knew practically nothing about journalism. But because I had done some writing, I was chosen to be the sports editor for the Baylor *Lariat*—a choice the faculty advisers later probably regretted.

I'll never forget the second day I was in journalism class. As our diminutive professor came walking into the classroom, I looked at him and thought, "He looks like a windup toy; I wonder if there's a key in his back." As Dr. Burkhalter spoke, his almost lipless mouth opened and shut much like a ventriloquist's dummy. His well-worn tweed suit had a folded

22 / Too Good to Keep

newspaper in the right pocket and a note or two pinned under the left lapel with paper clips—reminders of things he was to do that day.

On this particular day Mr. Frank, as we called him, addressed himself to the class. "Young men and women, today I have one of the most serious missions of my whole life. I am to visit the president of the First National Bank of this city. My purpose in talking with him will be to express my profound concern for his soul's salvation. He doesn't quite realize the necessity of conversion, but if you will pray, and I will be faithful in my witness, perhaps he will be turned to our blessed Saviour. And now, students, I would like you to covenant with me to pray as I go to witness to this very influential gentleman." He then bowed his head and led the whole class in prayer for the conversion of the president of the bank.

It blew my mind. I had never heard an adult man talk about witnessing to a bank president or to anyone else of that caliber. I thought that only a few people in the church witnessed, and then to children and young people. My heart pounded in my chest as I prayed for the conversion of the bank president.

The next day in class Dr. Burkhalter began by saying, "Ladies and gentlemen, I want to give a report of my stewardship of witness to the president of the bank yesterday. At first he did not want to receive Christ as his Saviour. He expressed to me that he was good enough already and had no need for personal salvation. I quoted Isaiah 53:6, 'All we like sheep have gone astray; we have turned everyone to his own way; and the Lord hath laid on Him the iniquity of us all.' I then read Romans 3:10 and 23 to Him: 'There is none righteous, no, not one.... For all

People Who Discovered It Could Be Done / 23

have sinned, and come short of the glory of God.' I told him that the word *all* definitely includes presidents of banks, and that he must not think of conversion as something needed only by men on skid row.

"Then he said, 'But I'm not a sinner.'

"I quoted 1 John 1:10 which says, 'If we say that we have not sinned, we make Him [God] a liar.'

"I asked him if he thought God was a liar.

"He said, 'No, of course not.'

"'If He is not, then you are a sinner because God says that all have sinned.'

"He said, 'Well, I have not sinned much; I'm not a wicked sinner.'

"I asked him what a wicked sinner was. He replied, 'One who has committed great sins and done terrible deeds.'

"I then told him Jesus' words: 'Thou shalt love the Lord thy God with all thy heart, and with all thy soul, and with all thy mind' (Matthew 22:37-38). I asked him if he loved God that way.

"He bowed his head and said, 'No, I guess not. I have not loved God as I should.'

"I told him about the terrible consequences of sin, showing him Galatians 3:10, 'Cursed is every one that continueth not in all things which are written in the book of the law to do them.' I asked him if he had done all the things that were written in the Word of God.

"He said, 'No, of course not.'

"I asked, 'Then what does the Scripture say is true of you?'

"He looked at the verse and said,'I am cursed because it says "Cursed is every one that continueth not in all things. . ."'

"I indicated to him that the Law demands a perfect and faithful obedience. That the man who fails to render perfect obedience is under the curse. That is to say, he is separated, banished from God. By this time my friend said he realized the depth of his sin, so he and I prayed together and he received Jesus Christ as his personal Saviour."

It is impossible to relate the depth of emotion that registered in my impressionable young soul as I watched this ordinary looking man. I was amazed at his power as a witness.

Dr. Frank Burkhalter, professor of journalism at Baylor for many years, led hundreds of teenage boys to Jesus Christ. He kept a record of their lives, interests, hobbies, and attitudes toward study. He was an ordinary man who made himself available to the Lord.

Fred

I remember Fred, an electrician. For 20 years, he taught a Sunday School class of 14-year-old boys at the First Baptist Church of Owensboro, Kentucky. Fred had a style all his own. He would teach the lesson and then ask one or two of the boys to stand up and tell the rest of the class the essence of the lesson he had taught. Fred led these young men to give their lives to Jesus Christ and to develop their art of speaking out for Jesus. When Fred left this earth, he left scores of young men won to Jesus Christ and several of them in the ministry. Fred was a talent scout for Christ. When he found young boys who had great potential, he led them to understand that there was one man who cared for their future. None of them escaped the influence of Fred's life. I was very happy to be Fred's pastor.

L.T.

I remember L.T. who worked for the Texas Gas and Transmission Company. He had come up the hard way in the gas and oil business. When he moved to our church in Owensboro, Kentucky, he asked for a conference with me as soon as he got established in his home and his job. The purpose of the conference was to discover if I knew any unique ways to win people to Jesus Christ. He had a loose-leaf Bible in which he recorded soul-winning techniques, and verses that meant much to him. His entire Bible became a manual on witnessing.

L.T. and I became fast friends. He would call and tell me, "I have a fish nibbling. Pray that he will bite soon. He is a man addicted to alcohol and is about to lose his job." Or, "I have a couple with whom I am to visit tonight. They need to know Jesus Christ. The only thing wrong with their marriage is that they're building it upon themselves and not the Lord."

He called me one night saying that one of his best friends was dying in the hospital. He was unsaved. I offered to go and try to reach him for Jesus Christ. L.T. said, "No, Pastor, you're the shepherd. Let this old sheep do some of the reproducing. I'm going to win him tonight because I've prayed for him for 15 years, and now this is his last chance. He won't see tomorrow." I called L.T. the next morning and he said, "Bill gave his life to Jesus about 10 o'clock last night. He died this morning at 8:15."

I remember the growing influence L.T. had with the laymen in our church. More than being a deacon, more than being an outstanding church leader, more than being a power on the finance committee, more than being a great Sunday School teacher, more than being a lay preacher, L.T. wanted to be a witness for

Jesus Christ. This was his chief aim and goal in life. The world is better because of L.T. Sloan.

Madge

I remember Madge, the wife of a lawyer in Palm Beach, Florida. She could have enjoyed all the fruits of wealth, but instead she chose to simply be a witness for Jesus Christ. She enjoyed teaching the Bible in one of our Sunday School classes, but more than that, she enjoyed winning people to Jesus Christ. She prayed for women and young people and won many of them to the Saviour.

One day Madge called me and asked if I would go with her to reach a woman who was 103 years old. All my life I had heard of people who became old and cold and uninterested in responding to anything concerning God and Christ.

When Madge and I arrived at the retirement hotel in Palm Beach, we went in to see Mrs. Graham. She was a wrinkled little lady, totally blind, sitting in a rocking chair. I talked with her for a while about the common matters of the day, and Madge looked at me as if to say, "Get on with it, Doc."

Finally I said, "Mrs. Graham, you've lived almost all of your life. Have you found the great secret of eternal life which will make it possible for you to rejoice with friends and loved ones again, and to live forever in happiness?"

Mrs. Graham said, "I'm afraid I have not learned that secret." So, sitting there at her feet like a child, holding her wrinkled hands in mine, I spoke to her simply and lovingly, about the Saviour. I saw tears come into her eyes.

When I asked her if she would like to receive Jesus as her Saviour and Lord, she leaped at it and said,

"Yes, that's what I've been waiting for all my life." Madge and I, our eyes full of tears, shared a salvation prayer with Mrs. Graham as she gave her life away to the Saviour. I will always be grateful for Madge.

Frank

I remember Frank, a car dealer in West Palm Beach. He was a stooped shouldered, friendly con artist. One day I drove by his place to talk with him about a car for my wife. Frank had drunk enough alcohol to float a Palm Beach yacht. And I was reminded of the night he nearly destroyed a Palm Beach night club, and then had three fist fights as he walked across the bridge from Palm Beach to West Palm Beach. He was a tough customer, a hustler after the dollar. There seemed very little hope that this man could ever do much for Christ.

Frank asked me to come into his little office where we could talk about the car I was interested in. When we sat down, he told me that Joe Vandegriff, the minister of evangelism from our church, had stopped to see him the day before and had told him about Jesus Christ. Tears came to Frank's eyes as he said, "Do you think God can use a no-good, hunch-backed con artist like me?"

I said, "Frank, He can use you if you'll give yourself to Him. Will you do it now?"

Frank said, "Not right now, I want to pray about it." Usually I would say, "Boast not thyself of tomorrow, for thou knowest not what a day may bring forth," but I did not to him—I felt impressed to give him the 24 hours.

During the night he talked with Joe Vandegriff again, and gave his life to Jesus Christ. His conversion resulted in an immediate and total transformation. Frank Nolan was afire for God. He made restitution everywhere he could, with people with whom he had made bad deals. Customers would be told about Christ before they would be shown a car.

When I asked him one day if a certain car was a good one, he said, "It would have been an excellent car if you and Joe Vandegriff had not led me to Jesus and Jesus had not taken the liar out of me. Actually, it's a pile of junk and I'm going to flush it through the auction. I wouldn't sell it to my worst enemy."

Some years later, Frank became chairman of the deacons at the First Baptist Church of West Palm Beach, Florida. I asked him to give his testimony one Sunday morning on television. He did and the entire congregation was shaken. There were many tears—and many souls that day. A lawyer in Palm Beach contacted me. He said, "I've been listening to you preach on television for several years. I have been able to answer every argument you've ever put forth on behalf of the Gospel of Christ, but last Sunday I heard and saw something I cannot answer. I knew Frank Nolan before he became a Christian, and now I know Frank Nolan since he became a Christian. The one thing in all these years that I have not been able to answer is the radical change in Frank Nolan's life." So the lawyer gave his life to Jesus Christ.

When we were building the new sanctuary of the First Baptist Church, a giant cross was put atop the tall steeple that towered above the inner coastal canal and the open ocean out of Palm Beach. They were about to hoist the cross and put it on top of the steeple when Frank raised his hand and said, "Just a minute, please." The little man dashed up to the cross and clambered to the top, took out his fountain pen and wrote his name, and then gave the signal to raise the cross high in the sky. Frank said, "It's just a symbol, but I wanted the Lord Jesus, when He comes down to look at the top of the cross, to know just exactly where I stand. When God looks down, He'll know that Frank's life was nailed to the cross with Jesus."

For most people that would have been overly sentimental, but Frank's quietness in that moment led me to realize that it was a totally sincere action. The authority of His amateurs is a power God uses.

I was on vacation when I received the message— "Frank Nolan died last night." I flew back to West Palm Beach on the loneliest flight of my life. When I arrived, my heart was in my throat, because I loved Frank so much. His funeral was a triumph. For sprinkled throughout that crowd were trophies of grace whom Frank Nolan had won to Jesus Christ. Every one of those men vowed to pick up the torch where Frank had left off. I saw the lawyer sitting in the far back of the room—he wept the most. Yes, I remember Frank.

Ronnie

I remember Ronnie, the pastor's son. He was nine. I was preaching a revival at the Parkside Baptist Church in Dennison, Texas, and the meeting was not going well. We were deeply burdened that something dramatic would happen to revolutionize the spirit of that church, and to encourage the laymen to come alive for witnessing. There was a dearth of interest in soul-winning. We had a prayer meeting each morning, and again and again I heard them praying for "Big Duke." I didn't know who Big Duke was, but I knew there was a burden in that community for his conversion.

One afternoon Ronnie came home from school. His mother knew something strange was happening because he took a bath! When Ronnie put on his Sunday School best, his mother asked, "Ronnie, what are you doing?"

"I've heard the whole town praying for Big Duke, but I've never heard of anyone going to talk with him." Ronnie's mother, a beautiful Christian, sensed the boy's intensity and did not interfere.

The little boy picked up his Sunday School Bible and went to Big Duke's house. Big Duke came to the door in his khakis and no shirt. "What do you want?" Duke bellowed out.

Ronnie said, "Mr. Duke, I have heard the people at the church praying for your conversion and I've come to talk to you about your soul's salvation."

Big Duke stared at him for a long time; then he said, "Well, I'll say one thing for you, kid, you've got guts. Come on in." The boy sat down, took out his Bible, and explained the simple plan of salvation, which his father and mother had taught him. For the first time in his life Big Duke found himself listening to the words from the Bible. The Scriptures were fired at him by a nine-year-old boy, but the effect was that of a cannon.

When Ronnie finished, Big Duke shrugged if off by saying, "Well, it was nice of you to come and I appreciate your interest. I will see you again sometime, I hope."

Ronnie said, "Mr. Duke, I promised the Lord that I not only would tell you about Jesus but would take you to church with me tonight."

"Not a chance, boy."

"Mr. Duke, you're lost, you're on the road to hell. I don't want you to be lost, because I've learned to love you. You just don't know how much power you could have in this town if you'd give your life to Jesus Christ."

"Not a chance, boy."

"Mr. Duke, I'm not leaving this house until you get yourself dressed and come with me to church tonight."

"Well, you're a persistent little blankety-blank, and I always have respected courage, so I'll come with you, but that's all."

The pastor's mouth fell open when he saw his son walk into the building with Big Duke. The whole church expected the plaster to fall, but it didn't. I stood up and preached a simple Gospel sermon and as passionately as I knew how, gave an appeal filled with expectancy and hope. I asked all who had not received Christ to come and make their profession of faith that night.

When the invitation began, Ronnie stepped out into the aisle like an usher in a theater. He turned to Big Duke and pointed down the aisle. Big Duke stared at me; his eyes turned to the pastor; he looked down at Ronnie. All of a sudden he broke up like a hard winter; tears began coursing down his cheeks, and Big Duke walked down the aisle giving his life away to Jesus Christ.

As I hugged this strong man, I gave silent thanks for Ronnie, a courageous nine-year-old.

Bill

I remember Bill who was born with a horrible birthmark across his face. It was one of those dark purple blotches that made people shudder when they met him. Bill had other problems. He was very slow of speech. His movements were uncoordinated, and he appeared to be far less intelligent than he actually was.

I was preaching a crusade in the city of Nashville. At the close of the first evening service in the War Memorial Auditorium, this young man walked up to me and asked me if he could talk with me. I postponed a dinner engagement with friends, telling them I would be there in a short while. Then I sat down to talk with Bill.

"Dr. Moody," he said, "a lot of people don't think God can use me to win souls to Jesus Christ. Do you think God could use me to win someone?"

Deep down inside, the cold logic of my mind said, *No, not in a thousand years could this person become effective.* But I spoke by faith and not by sight, as I said, "Bill, it has always been my belief that any human being who will make himself available to Jesus Christ can win someone else to the Saviour."

A smile swept across Bill's face; it was a crooked smile. His slurred speech touched me as he said, "I am so glad you told me I could win souls to Jesus Christ because lots of people tell me I can't. I know I'm not much to look at, but maybe my bad looks will make people look away from me and see Jesus." The logic of his statement did not escape me. For once, I found a rationale for all the ugly people of the world.

The next night I saw Bill sitting far back in the auditorium. Directly in front of him sat one of the most outstanding athletes in the city. He was a four-letter man, and a handsome cut of a young man. When I extended the invitation I saw Bill in his uncoordinated way move toward the tall athlete in front of him and whisper something. The young man shook his head. Then Bill whispered something else and I saw the young man start making his way to the aisle. When that young athlete came to the front of the auditorium and gave his life to Christ, right behind him, tears coursing down his purple face, was Bill Aspermont. That week Bill won half a dozen people to Jesus Christ. There was something about his humility, something about his style, something about his insistence, that made me realize God can use anyone.

Sometime later I prayed, "Dear God, I do not ask that you make me another Spurgeon, or that you make me another George Truett or Billy Graham. But, dear God, I do request that somehow, in your divine economy of grace, it be possible that I become another Bill Aspermont."

The World Is Waiting for You

These stories are true. The purpose of writing them is to convey the fact that the eternal God is not looking for unusual people to do unusual things. He is looking for very ordinary people to make themselves available, so that Christ can be about the extraordinary work of world revolution by changing people one by one.

The world is waiting for you. God wants you to go into His world—the world in which you live—to the people with whom you have dialogue every day, and simply and quietly share what God has done in and through your life.

In memory of Mr. Frank, Fred, L.T., Madge, Frank, Ronnie, and Bill, I urge you to believe deeply that there is no limitation upon you but your own unwillingness to respond to God's claim upon your life. God has been ready for a long time; He is ready for you now. Be willing to try, and God will cause you to lead people to Jesus Christ.

I can see you now leading people to Christ and bringing them to church Sunday after Sunday, escorting them down the aisle to the Saviour who loves them so. I can see you winning 50 souls a year, one a week, because you have systematically disciplined yourself to talk face to face with one person per day.

Would you join with me in claiming at least one soul led to Christ and introduced to your pastor and your church every week? Would you claim with me God's living presence as you try to share your faith with at least one person per day? It only takes 15 minutes per day to talk to a lost person about Jesus Christ. Your pastor will be delighted to give you the names of unconverted people in your town. You know hundreds of them personally. If you will cultivate your eyes to see "the fields white unto harvest" now waiting for you to come and reap the harvest, God will give the increase for which you pray. There are many happy people in this world, but the happiest people I know are those who systematically lead people to Jesus Christ.

Look at your watch. What time is it? Would you be willing, before your watch ticks another 60 seconds, to have written down the name of one unsaved person, to have called him and asked him for an appointment to discuss a matter of very great importance? Tell him you want to talk with him privately, and need only 15-20 minutes of his time. If by the end of the next hour you have done this, you'll be shocked at how clean and right and joyous you will begin to feel. And tomorrow when you see him, go in the boldness of God because, "All authority has been given unto me in heaven and in earth. Go ye therefore."

People Who Discovered It Could Be Done / 35

The authority of God is back of you, so walk tall; don't be afraid. Ask God to give you some spine. Brush up on a few verses of Scripture to show him. Be his friend, love him, let him know you love his soul—probably no one in all his life has ever told him that he loves his soul. This may be the first time that he will ever hear those golden words. Then show him the ABC's of salvation:

A—Romans 3:23, "*All* have sinned and come short of the glory of God."
B—Acts 16:31, "*Believe* on the Lord Jesus Christ and thou shalt be saved."
C—Romans 10:9-10, "That if thou shalt *confess* with thy mouth the Lord Jesus and shalt believe in thine heart that God hath raised him from the dead, thou shalt be saved."

Explain these three verses of Scripture as clearly as you know how. You prayed before you witnessed. Now, having witnessed, commit it to Christ, and boldly urge your friend to give His life to Jesus Christ. He may or may not accept Christ immediately, but he will not forget the fact that you came, that you cared, that you shared. It may be a month, it may be a year, but the seed you sow tomorrow in that specific appointment will bear fruit. God's Word will not return unto Him void. You can count on that. If you don't believe it, remember Frank, Fred, L.T., Madge, Frank, Ronnie, and Bill.

FOUR
"How Do I Begin?"

I will never forget the first person I won to Jesus Christ. I was 17 years of age and I didn't know how to do it. My dear friend was Frank Shannon, who had never received Christ as his Saviour. I lived at Frank's house half the time, and he lived at my house half the time. We were on the same football team and we were buddies. Frank was a beautiful, blonde, freckled Irishman, as strong as a bear. One night in my house, Frank and I were sitting in the living room talking. I looked at him and said, "Frank, I don't know how to tell you, I don't know what to do. I just want you to know that Jesus Christ has become very real to me lately, and I've given my life to Him. Frank, I want you to give your life to Him too."

Frank said, "Golly, what do I do?"

I said, "Frank, I don't know what to tell you to do. I just know that Jesus died for me and I know that He died for you. I know I believe on Jesus and He saved my life and satisfies me, and I want you to do the same thing.

Frank said, "How do I do it?"

I said, "I don't know, but let's just bow our heads and tell God all about it."

Frank bowed his head and said, "God, I don't know what words to say. I just know I want to say the right words to You because I want You to know that I really do love You, and I want to give my life to Your Son, Jesus." Frank stopped praying and looked up at me and said, "Is that it?"

I said, "I'm asking you. Is that it?"

Frank's face lit up and he said, "Yeah, that's it." And he took my hand.

Mind you, I led a soul to Jesus Christ and I didn't quote one verse of Scripture. All I shared was an experience.

If you think about this experience with Frank, you'll see something very important. Simon Peter did not have a New Testament when he preached the sermon at Pentecost. Philip did not have a New Testament when he won the eunuch. Paul did not have a New Testament when he preached the Gospel around the Mediterranean world. The only things the early church had to go on were Old Testament promises that the Messiah would come and their experience with Jesus Christ. They shared that which they had experienced and won thousands upon thousands of people to Christ.

If Jess Moody at 17 years of age—not knowing one verse of Scripture or one hymn, but knowing he had had an experience with the Lord—could win Frank Shannon to Jesus Christ, then you can do it too.

Begin With People
"Where do I begin?" With people. Where they are in their world.

Think of the stories that Jesus told. Most often they

had to do with money and property—the pearl of great price, the rich man and Lazarus, the lost coin, the lost sheep, the widow's mite, the wheat and the tares, the good and the bad soil, the rich young ruler, the unfruitful fig tree. His stories were of consuming interest to poor, deprived people. He started exactly at the center of their interest and led them to the center of His interest. The weather, athletic events, fashions, automobiles, hobbies, or the developing of a skill—all have been used with great effectiveness by soul-winners to lead others to Jesus Christ. We must start where people's interests are.

When I was a high schooler I had but one athletic skill—the ability to throw the forward pass. Outside of that one talent I was a triple threat: stumble, fumble, and fall. But I could throw accurately and at great distances. Sammy Baugh was my idol and I patterned my throwing skill after that ancient pioneer of the forward pass. To my mind he was the greatest football player who ever lived, everything considered.

One twelve-year-old boy I met much later dreamed of becoming another Bob Griese. This lad was tall, had a good arm and a good eye, but he didn't know how to grip the ball. There was a fallacy in the release of the ball from his hands and fingers that made it go awry just a little bit. I showed him the Sammy Baugh grip and told him it was different from the grip employed by most, and that it had worked for me in the long ago. I showed him how to release the ball from the hand and from the fingers. I showed him how to lead the receiver just enough to put it in his hands, what kind of pass to throw if there was a defensive man between him and the receiver, or if the defensive man was on the other side of the receiver or coming in from the right or the left. I taught him when to throw the high lob, the soft pass, when to rifle it, and when to give it just the right touch.

After catching and throwing with Ricky for a couple of hours, he came to me and said, "Are you really a preacher?" I considered that a great compliment. I think somewhere in his past, he picked up the idea that preachers didn't get the hiccups or toothaches, or have to wash behind their ears. Somehow my humanity and his humanity had met. After that, I was able to talk to him about Jesus and he accepted Christ as his Saviour.

In intramural games, I've had the privilege of leading to Christ some of the young men with whom I played. I was still playing when I was 43 years of age and nearly holding my own with those young bucks. But I'll tell you something. Before my 16-year ministry in West Palm Beach was over, every boy but one had received Jesus Christ as his Saviour and was active in the church.

I remember Pop Halbert who was pastor of the Harbor Baptist Church in Houston. Pop Halbert had been vice-president of Continental Can, and late in life gave his life to the ministry. He took a small church in the rough harbor district of Houston. He built a great little church there and was used mightily until the day of his death. Pop Halbert sat down with many aspiring young men, and taught them all the business know-how he had accumulated through the years. But strangely enough, every young man with whom he spent time ended up an active, praying, witnessing, tithing Christian, loyal to his church, and loyal to Christ.

The strategic use of what you know other than the

Scriptures will often lead men and women to a knowledge of the Lord. I've seen welders lead young welders-in-training to Christ; women using tennis or golf as a means to witness, men using their civic club relationships as opportunities for witnessing about their Lord.

I remember a young lawyer who won several to Christ as the result of developing relationships with them by playing handball. Anything—the love of flowers, the love of birds, bicycling, motorcycling, sailing, hiking, mountain climbing, sales meetings—all of these are springboards of witnessing. What one must do is develop the eye to see the witness nestling in the palm of a secular situation. It is always there; in fact, it is more often there than it is in the church building. The world will sit up and take notice when we Christians sit up and take notice of what makes the world sit up and take notice.

Begin With Yourself
"But where do I begin in witnessing? How do I do it?"

● Make sure you are born from above. You cannot tell someone else about Jesus Christ if you have not had that personal experience yourself. You must be born again. If you've only been born of the flesh, all you can do is tell them fleshly experiences. But if you've been born of the Spirit, you can tell them spiritual experiences. So believe on Jesus Christ as your personal Saviour. Get that settled! Settle it right now and don't wait a minute about it! "Believe on the Lord Jesus Christ and thou shalt be saved" (Acts 16:31). Fall to your knees right now and ask Christ to become your Saviour. He will save you the minute you ask Him. Repent, which means to change your attitude about the Gospel, open yourself up to the Gospel, and then receive Christ.

Don't receive the Gospel, don't receive the plan of salvation, don't receive a sermon, don't receive "God," but open your life and ask Jesus Christ, God's way of salvation, to come into your heart and life, forgive you of your sins. Then publically confess that you have given your life to Jesus Christ. Be baptized in the name of the Father, Son, and Holy Spirit. Then you are ready to tell others about Jesus Christ.

● Provide a willing attitude. You must be willing to be led of the Holy Spirit to go out to see unconverted people.

● Ask your pastor for a list of names of unsaved people, or talk with your minister of education. Or if your church has a soul-winning program in it, go to the leader of that program and ask him to give you names, because you want to start today witnessing for Jesus Christ. There will be those who will attempt to tell you that you need a one-year course before you're ready to talk to people about Jesus Christ as Saviour and Lord.

It is true that good training does more than poor training to enable a person to serve the Lord in every capacity, but soul-winning is the sharing of an experience.

● If you have had an experience with Jesus Christ, find someone and tell him about your experience. Don't be a lapel grabber; don't overly insist, don't stay too long.

Say something like this: "Look, John, I don't know how to do what I'm attempting to do, but all I know is I've received Jesus Christ as my personal Saviour and He completely satisfies me. I've come to your house tonight to sit down and look you in the eye and ask you if you would like to receive Jesus Christ as your Saviour the way I did. I promise you, John, Jesus will meet every need of your life and you will never be the same. Will you receive Jesus Christ right now? I will lead you in a prayer that you can repeat after me. 'Dear God, I know that I am a sinner, I know I cannot save myself. I know Jesus died to save me from my sins, and I now receive Jesus as my Saviour and my Lord. Thank You, Lord, for saving me from my sin. In Jesus name, Amen.'"

Then look John in the eye and say, "John, I know you prayed that prayer with me, didn't you?"

And 99 times out of 100 he will say, "Yes, I did."

Then rejoice, get excited, and say, "John, you're saved, isn't that wonderful?" Get so excited about it that you just can't contain yourself. Tell John's wife, tell the family, get on the phone and call John's mother and tell her that tonight John received Jesus Christ as his Saviour.

After the excitement has settled down a little bit, tell him, "John, I want you to come with me to church next Sunday, I want to sit with you, and you and I are going to walk down the aisle together and you are going to publicly confess that you received Jesus into your heart and you'll be baptized into the church family. Then you and I will tell others about this wonderful thing that has happened to you. John, I want you to tell everyone you meet. Will you tell your secretary? Don't let anything hold you back. This is the most important thing in the world, John, and I'm so thrilled that you've received Christ."

Then after you walk out of his home, sit down in your car, bow your head, open your heart, and cry out to God: "God, there's one. Just think, in this country there are only 140 million to go."

"How Do I Begin?" / 43

If you are a member of a Bible teaching church, you know the facts of sin, that Christ died for sin, that sin abounds everywhere, and that all men are sinners. You know that man is in need of a Saviour, and that Jesus Christ is the Saviour who came.

You know the story of the serpent, the devil, the liar. You know that Satan is the Prince of the Power of the Air, the Adversary, the Dragon, and you know that disobedience came by one man, Adam.

You know the results of sin—the curse upon the serpent, the sorrow to the woman, labor for man. All kinds of evidences abound that sin is around us; the curse is everywhere.

You know that God's plan, Jesus Christ, makes reaching people possible—you know all of these things. So it isn't necessary for you to learn anything more about theology to become a soul-winner. All you have to know is that Jesus Christ died for sinners, that all men are sinners, and that all men must be told, for Jesus said, "Go to them."

For you to take another course in theology to learn anything more is not immediately necessary. Any truck driver, dishwasher, photographer, pilot, or farmer can become a great soul-winner. Remember what happened when you were saved? Jesus provided the Saviour, and you provided the sinner; therefore, you are saved.

Now, Jesus has told you how to go out into the world and preach the Gospel. All you are to do is provide the soul-winner and He will provide the saving of souls.

I maintain that anyone, anywhere, can win souls to Jesus Christ. It is the central commitment of the church of Jesus Christ.

FIVE
"How Do I Present the Gospel?"

One of the most serious mistakes I made, as a young Christian, was to assume that the people to whom I witnessed knew more about the Gospel than they actually did. This is a serious and soul-killing error.

While most people *think* they know God's specific plan of salvation, close examination reveals that their minds are full of distortions. Some of the chief distortions are: salvation by *good works*, salvation by *baptism*, salvation by *church membership*, salvation by *intermediary*, salvation by *universal grace*, salvation by *religion*, salvation by *honesty*.

There are hundreds of ramifications of these, any of which may lurk in the recesses of the mind and not manifest themselves in conversation. They need to be ferreted out and eliminated. And only one method—courteous, respectful Bible teaching—will produce this desired result.

I have discovered that witty put-downs to the other person are the chief enemy of effectively reaching that person. Wit and humor are always welcome in a conversation, but never when they reduce the other person's viewpoint to the absurd. His view may *be* absurd, but I must guard against making him feel resentful at me because I have attacked his intelligence for holding a contrary opinion.

When a witness realizes that his prospect holds to a false hope, the best thing to do is to third-person the situation. This is done in two steps. First, let a little time pass after the prospect reveals the false salvation prop to which he is clinging. Then, tell of another person who believed the same thing and later worked out of that viewpoint into a true reliance upon Christ as his only hope. This technique eliminates the sensation of frontal attack.

The Person and Work of Jesus Christ

The old saying goes something like this: "You can't tell what you haven't learned anymore than you can come from where you've never been."

It is true that one cannot share what he doesn't know and hasn't experienced. What then are the basic facts a witness should know?

The first truth is that *salvation comes in no other way than through the person and work of Jesus Christ*. "Neither is there salvation in any other; for there is none other name under heaven given among men, whereby we must be saved" (Acts 4:12).

This eliminates all other concepts of salvation. We are not saved by good works, baptism, confession to an intermediary, church membership, or religion, but only through Jesus Christ.

To His disciples, Jesus said, "I am the way, the truth, and the life. No man cometh to the Father but by Me" (John 14:6). Human beings send up thousands of religious forms, but God sent *down* only one way, and it wasn't a religion. It was His Son.

"For God so loved the world that He gave His only begotten Son, that whosoever believeth in Him should not perish but have everlasting life" (John 3:16). No verse better explains the Gospel.

The Gospel begins with God.
> **For God**

The Gospel is God's loving nature.
> **so loved**

The Gospel is a universal Gospel.
> **the world**

The Gospel is God's giving nature.
> **that He gave**

The Gospel is God giving His best.
> **His only begotten Son**

The Gospel is for everyone, everywhere.
> **that whosoever**

The Gospel is made operative by faith.
> **believeth**

The Gospel is faith in a Person.
> **in Him**

The Gospel protects from death.
> **should not perish**

The Gospel provides life forever.
> **but have everlasting life.**

The fact that God sent His only begotten Son raises another major question: *Why was the Gospel necessary?* God's Word answers clearly: *Because of sin.* The most familiar verse on the subject of man's sinfulness is Romans 3:23: "For all have sinned, and come short of the glory of God."

The context of this verse is seldom studied, but the verses immediately preceding Romans 3:23 are a treasure trove for understanding the nature of man.

Jew and Gentile are all under sin	v. 9.
No one is righteous, not one	v. 10.
No one understands or seeks God	v. 11.
Everyone has gone the wrong way	v. 12.
Everyone is unprofitable	v. 12.
Not one does good	v. 12.
Everyone speaks deceit, cursing, bitterness	vv. 13-14.
Everyone wants to shed blood	v. 15.
Everyone walks toward destruction and misery	v. 16.
No one knows the way of peace	v. 17.
No one fears God	v. 18.
Every man is guilty before the law	v. 19.
No one can justify himself	v. 20.
Everyone can be saved by God's righteousness	v. 21.
This righteousness is through Jesus Christ	v. 22.

The logic is inescapable. Man, the total sinner, needs total salvation. A totally loving God sends the total remedy for sin in Jesus Christ.

A serious analysis of Romans 3 will reveal Paul's complete mistrust in man's righteousness and an absolute trust in the righteousness of God.

These two facts—Man's sinfulness and God's righteousness—form the framework of the salvation message.

An exhaustive theological study will take one full circle to arrive again at the simple fact that "God sent His Son to be the Saviour of the world."

A Person, Not a Plan

There are several tracts which present clear summations of the Gospel. Some of the most widely used are: "The Four Spiritual Laws" (Campus Crusade), "The Full and Meaningful Life" (Southern Baptist Convention), and "The Happiness Book" (First Baptist Church, Van Nuys, California).

There is one point that an effective personal evangelist must always bear in mind when using a tract: People are not saved by a plan; they are saved by a Person. In sharing one's faith, one must never say, "Do you believe what this tract says?" but "Do you believe in this Person, Jesus Christ?"

Only Christ, the perfect Lamb of God, slain from the foundation of the world, can save.

Only the eternal Son of God, who became incarnate in the flesh by the Holy Spirit, can save.

Only this Person, who perfectly revealed and did the will of God when taking upon Himself the demands of human nature, who identified with mankind yet never sinned, can save.

Only He who honored God's law by His personal obedience, and by His death on the cross made provision for the redemption of people from sin, can save.

Only the One who was raised from the dead with a glorified body, and appeared to His disciples as the Person who was with them before the crucifixion, can save.

Only He who ascended into heaven and is now exalted at the right hand of God the Father where He is the one Mediator, partaking of the nature of God and of man, in whose Person is effected the reconciliation between God and man, can save.

Only the One who will return in power and glory to judge the world and to consummate His redemptive mission, and who now dwells in all believers as the living and ever-present Lord, can save.

Some Plans for Witnessing

Any plan of salvation must point to the Saviour, the Person of salvation. I have used these simple presentations to reach people of every walk of life.

THE GOSPEL IN THREE MINUTES

A. "*ALL* have sinned and come short of the glory of God." Romans 3:23
(30-second explanation)

B. "BELIEVE on the Lord Jesus Christ and thou shalt be saved." Acts 16:31
(30-second explanation)

C. "CONFESS with your mouth the Lord Jesus and believe in your heart that God has raised Him from the dead and thou shalt be saved." Romans 10:9
(30-second explanation)

THE MOST IMPORTANT QUESTIONS IN THE WORLD

A. What is my most serious problem?
  - Sin—Romans 3:34; 6:23; Isaiah 53:6.

B. What can I do about it?
  - Repent—Acts 2:38; 26:20; Romans 2:4; 2 Peter 3:9. Genuinely turn from sin to God.
  - Believe—Acts 16:31. Accept Jesus Christ and commit my entire personality to Him, as my Lord and Saviour.
  - Confess—Romans 10:9-10.

Walk the aisle in a regular service of your church and tell the pastor that you have received Christ (or make it public by whatever means your church provides).

Be baptized in the Christian fellowship of your church.

Be faithful to the worship services and the Sunday School.

C. When should I do this?
- Right now. Right here. It isn't essential to be in a church.

The Ethiopian eunuch received Christ on a dusty road—Acts 8.

YOUR STORY

There are myriads of plans of salvation, but the best witness is to tell your own personal story. I know exactly what you are thinking. "Who would be interested in hearing about me?"

Only everybody. The world never tires of hearing one person's story. The writers know it. The movies know it. The church must learn it.

But how? Write it out.

First, the B.C.—what you were before Christ. Then, the birth of Christ in your life. Finally, the A.D.—what it has been since.

Go into detail, but don't drag it out. Work up three lengths: short—3 minutes; medium—10 minutes; and long—30 minutes.

Spend a lot of time preparing each of them. Make them sizzle. Emphasize the serious nature of your condition outside of Christ. Give the operation of grace in your life some heavy emphasis. What

"How Do I Present the Gospel?" / 51

happened? How did you feel when you received Christ? How did it affect you, your mate, your children, your parents, your schoolmates? What has happened since? Don't make it a perfect success story; tell them about your failures since you found Christ.

A sincere word of caution: Don't mess up your testimony with visions and the weird! Even if you walked on water, don't tell it. It will ruin the natural flow of the story of God's love moving in your life.

The more human, common, and natural it is, the more people who live common and natural lives will relate to it.

One of the most touching kinds of testimony is that which relates how a personal relationship was messed up and how finding Christ healed that relationship. This brings tears to my psyche everytime. How did finding Christ better the communication between you and your mate? Your father or mother? Your children? How did Christ heal your memories, the bitterness of old hatreds and hangups?

I can see you now telling in a natural, loving, humble way, your Christ story. Every person is a three-act play: B.C., Christ's triumphal entry into your life, and A.D.

I can imagine the feeling that floods through your body and spirit when you see a tear in a friend's eye as he listens to you share your faith.

The first time may make your knees shake a little but it will get easier. The first three minutes will be the toughest.

I have made an exhaustive study and it is a fact of history: No one has ever died from nerves while giving a Christian testimony! Several have *thought* they were going to expire from fright while testifying—but no one ever has.

What will others think of you? They'll think, "I wish I had a testimony like that," or "I'm really proud of Mary—up there telling about Christ in her life." And, God willing, someone will say, "Lord, I'm coming home!"

SIX
Have a Gentle Attitude

The effective winner of men must be a good people reader. He must be intuitive in understanding the nuances of attitudes and movements of the person with whom he is sharing the Gospel. To be able to get into the home of a person is one thing. To understand that that home is the other man's castle, and is to be treated with respect and delicacy, is another thing. The wish of the host is the law of the guest and you are the guest. I have seen "soul-winners" who, having gained entrance into the home, become boorish, almost arrogant, and bewilderingly pushy. I have seen those same people literally ordered out of the home after the dialogue ended up in a harangue.

Steve

Steve, a fine young boy from our church in West Palm Beach, had vanished from our church about 10 years before. I inquired about him and learned that he had moved to another city. Now, 10 years later, two handsome young men asked for a conference with me. When they came into my office I discovered that one of them was Steve. He and his friend were Jehovah's Witnesses. His friend was an ardent debater, and I allowed him to make his complete presentation. Then I asked if I could give some answers to him. When I started giving reply, he became livid—a heaving mass of doctrinal diatribe. He literally inundated me with loud, abusive words.

Steve interrupted him and said, "Now, Bill, I want you to stop what you're doing; you're a poor witness for our cause because you've lost your temper. I love this man as a friend and know him to be very sincere in what he believes. You and I believe that he is mistaken, but he has shown a loving spirit toward you. And you're not showing the spirit that I feel in my heart toward this man whom I love and respect."

While Steve's doctrine was cultic, his attitude was as sound as a Swiss franc. The loving expectancy of friendship, of believing in the personal worth of a human being with whom you are talking—this is what wins men to Jesus, not witnessing formulas, not patent answers to their questions. The genuine, caring, respecting spirit toward the human person— this is the golden mean of witnessing.

Philip

Note the tact of Philip when he encountered the Ethiopian eunuch (Acts 8). When Philip saw that the eunuch was reading the Scriptures, he could have approached the man in numerous wrong ways, asking questions like,

"I'm sure you don't understand what you are reading, but I do, and I can teach you what it's all about."

"Are you saved, brother? That book will lead you to the Lord."

Have a Gentle Attitude / 55

"Are you a Christian?"

"Would you like to become a Christian?"

There are dozens of wrong ways to witness. For each individual, depending on his personality, there is usually only one right way.

Note what Philip said. He asked, "Do you understand what you're reading?" How tactful. How gentle. And the eunuch said, "How can I, seeing there is no one here to help me?" This was a gentle response of humility, an admission of ignorance. The result was that *later* Philip preached about Jesus to him, won him to Christ, and immediately baptized him.

There is no passage of Scripture where one accepted Christ and delayed being baptized. There were no indoctrination courses; they were baptized upon their profession of faith in Jesus Christ. That is all one needs to be a candidate for baptism.

History has it that the Ethiopian eunuch was the founder of the Coptic Church in Africa, of which there are millions of members. Imagine, all the way from one tactful question, "Do you understand what you are reading?" to the founding of churches of which there are millions of members. That is what tact can do. That is what courtesy can do. A gentle question can lead to some very ultimate answers and decisions.

Millions have been won to Jesus Christ by a good attitude; tragically, millions have been turned away from Him by a poor attitude. Carnal Christians should never witness; they have nothing to offer. Carnal Christians cannot be used by the Holy Spirit and they do more damage than good. The Spirit-filled Christian who has the fruit of the Spirit, love, demonstrated in his life, is always effective in bringing people to a saving knowledge of Jesus Christ.

Mr. Crouch

Once when I was a guest evangelist at a church in Kansas, I heard scores of prayer requests for a Mr. Crouch. Many were deeply burdened for his spiritual condition. I inquired why people were so concerned about him. They told me that he was probably the finest man in town. He never harmed anyone, always helped when a neighbor had a problem, and possessed a beautiful warm spirit. But he felt that he did not need anything other than his own morality to commend himself to God. The only time he ever became agitated was when people tried to share Christ with him.

Later that week I visited him in his home. He treated me cordially, and as we sat in his living room, I said, "Mr. Crouch, you're probably as moral a man as there is in this community. I've heard nothing but good about you. I've heard about your helping the Frasers when Mr. Fraser was ill, how you helped finish the back part of his house. This is so commendable.

"I realize I am a stranger, and strangers are not usually welcome to talk about delicate subjects. But Mr. Crouch, years ago in a clover field at 3 o'clock one morning I was called by the Lord to preach the Gospel. Several of my close friends died in World War II, and I was deeply bitter over that loss. But the tears of my sorrow became a telescope to see clearly the will of God for my life. He told me He wanted me to share the Gospel with everybody I could, and I want to share it with you. But if it will offend or upset you, if it will make you angry, I will delay until

Have a Gentle Attitude / 57

another time when you are ready to listen. I would like your permission to tell you very simply of the love God has for Mr. Crouch. Would you be willing for me to do that, without being offended?"

He shifted in his seat. I loved him with my eyes, my spirit and my voice. I intended no harm to him. I was wide open to help him. Somehow he seemed to know that I really cared about him and his own life's future.

"No, I won't be offended," he said. "I promise I won't."

So I told him, ever so gently, that we cannot be saved by our own good works. I told him that God was proud of every man's effort to do good. I didn't use the "filthy rags" approach concerning his good works. I commended him for his good works and told him that I believed God appreciated his attitude toward his neighbor, and that he fulfilled many Scriptures.

Then I felt led to take a different tack. I said, "Do you remember hearing the verse that talks about giving a cup of cold water in Jesus' name?" He did. "That verse about 'I was in prison and you visited Me?'" He said, "Yes." "And also 'Inasmuch as ye have done it unto the least of these, My brethren, ye have done it unto Me?'" He said, "Yes, that is one of my favorites."

"That's very good. I commend you for knowing those verses. But Mr. Crouch, it says 'a cup of cold water *given in My name.*' Now, you've been glad to give the cup of cold water, but it has always been given in Crouch's name. If you will accept Jesus as your personal Saviour, I'm sure our Lord will make it possible for every cup of cold water given by you in the future to be given in Christ's name. If you have not believed on His name, the good deeds you do are not done in Christ's name. (See Matthew 26.)

"Now, Mr. Crouch, wouldn't it be a terrible tragedy if all the things you've done for your neighbors were to go for nothing? For God loves a gentle spirit such as yours, loves an attitude such as yours. And the church needs the person who worships on Sunday morning and witnesses and helps in Jesus' name during the week.

"You see, there are people who say, 'Well, Mr. Crouch is not a Christian and yet he is the best man in town.' All your good deeds have become stumblingblocks for younger men in town. If they heard that you had given your heart to Jesus Christ, I'm sure they would turn to the Lord too. So the finest good deed you could ever do is to give those young men your example and help us lead them to the saving knowledge of Jesus Christ."

The Lord blessed that approach, and Mr. Crouch gave his heart to Jesus Christ. I was so grateful for that experience. It is one of my memory treasures.

Mary Lee

The best technique of all in winning souls to Jesus Christ is having a gentle, humble attitude toward those whose souls hang delicately in the balance. It is a technique which must be very sincerely used or it will appear to be more hypocritical than not. And if it isn't done sincerely, it will be hypocritical.

Once I was talking to a man in Batavia, New York about becoming a Christian, when his daughter, a very attractive and sophisticated and intelligent young lady, came into the room. I explained to her what I was doing. Immediately her countenance displayed anger. She said, "My father is an excellent

Have a Gentle Attitude / 59

man, a clean man, a moral man, and he doesn't need some bigot marching up to his house and trying to unsettle him and make him feel that he is less than a human being. I will thank you to leave him alone. He lives a better life than any of you hypocrites, and I just don't appreciate your being here at all."

I asked, "Mary Lee, may I say a word to you?" She folded her arms, crossed her legs, sat back in the chair, and answered, "All right, say what you have to say, but make it quick."

I said, "Mary Lee, years ago I felt that my good works commended me to God. I felt that I could go to heaven on the basis of my good works because the mass media had told me this. I had seen it in the movies and heard it from the man on the street. But the Bible, a Book which men have tried to destroy for centuries, a Book which is God's love-letter to the world explaining His love plan for all mankind, tells me that we are not saved by our good works."

I quoted Ephesians 2:8-9, "For by grace are ye saved through faith, and that not of yourself, it is the gift of God not of works, lest any man should boast."

I then said something like this: "I'm in the city for only a few days, and it is very difficult for me to talk to strangers. But your father is such a good man and such an outstanding man in this community, I really want him and his influence to count for Jesus Christ. And, Mary Lee, you are a beautiful, intelligent person. I would love to see you join your father. I can see you now, with your good mind, teaching a Sunday School class of young people in the church. I can see those young people being inspired by your wit and wisdom. I can see your beautiful life testifying that Jesus Christ has changed your life and made you a valuable instrument in His hands. I can see those young people being changed and some of them becoming Christian doctors and lawyers, and some of them Christian school teachers influencing thousands of children, and some of them becoming missionaries and pastors, because today, in your living room, you gave your life to Jesus Christ. I can really see that, Mary Lee, and I would love to see you and your father join with me in the acceptance of this wonderful Saviour."

I noticed her arms were unfolded, her legs uncrossed, and that a tear had come to her eyes. She said, "Please forgive me for being bitter. I've had such a terrible day. I hope you'll forgive me."

I said, "Mary Lee, I love you. I want you to give your life to Jesus Christ. There's nothing for me to forgive because I'm not in the forgiving business. Christ is the forgiver."

I'm happy to say that both of them gave their lives to Jesus Christ that day.

SEVEN
Don't Be Afraid

I've seen all kinds of church members who have won souls to Jesus Christ-fat ones, thin ones, tall ones, short ones, huge rolling mastodon types. Anyone can win people to Jesus Christ.

Jessie Cummins, my mother-in-law, was one of the most nervous public speakers that I've ever known. She was extremely tense while standing before an audience. About 25 years ago when she decided that the Great Commission was her responsibility, she went to her pastor, Judson Prince of the Riverside Baptist Church in Fort Worth, Texas, and told him that she couldn't speak to a group but that she wanted to start knocking on doors for Jesus Christ. She asked no salary.

For 20 years Jessie Cummins visited hundreds of people each month—the sick, the lonely, the frightened, the neurotic, the wealthy, the affluent, the kids living together without marriage, the alcoholic, the drug addict, the family that had just lost their child, the old man alone in his rocking chair watching TV. Hundreds of people were witnessed to by a woman who was too frightened to stand in front of a group and speak. I've known her to do things she did not want to do simply because it was a command of Jesus. And that's just the point!

You simply must do God's will, whether you like it or not, whether it is convenient or not, whether it is raining, snowing, or too hot. That doesn't matter. The responsibility is yours and you must obey or you are out of the will of God. And you're going to lose reward after reward—rewards here on earth, and rewards in heaven. What a terrible loss Christians undergo when they refuse to obey the commands of Christ.

E. Stanley Jones tells the story of a missionary woman who took little abandoned girls into her home. This woman lived in China at a time when many parents did not want girl children. To begin with, she had 1 girl, then 2 then 3 then 10 ... 20 ... 40. And for many, many years she fed, clothed, and cared for hundreds of unwanted little children. She taught them the Christian Gospel and made them into responsible human beings. When she died, on her tombstone were written these words: "She hath done what she couldn't."

I am certain she did not relish the idea of caring for those children, but Jesus had said unto her, "Inasmuch as you have done it unto one of the least of these ... you have done it unto Me" (Matthew 25:40). So she did what she could not do.

Don't Be Afraid to Give Your Best

Don't be afraid to give your best to Jesus, however insignificant you think it is. Whatever you give to Jesus will never be enough, as far as you are concerned. But no matter how small it is, it will be plenty as far as He is concerned. Your giving will be based on your partial knowledge of God and of yourself. His receiving will be based on His complete knowledge of Himself and of you.

Mary Magdalene offered Jesus a precious gift—a pound of ointment, costly spikenard—with which she anointed His feet. She was not afraid to give her best to Him.

Mary did not fully realize who Jesus was. Her motives were not totally spiritual and pure, as she anointed His feet and dried them with her hair. But she came to Him unashamedly in an act that indicated a total giving of herself to Him.

The big story here is that although Mary offered a gift that was not enough, and which was based on very mixed motives, Jesus received the offering as being complete.

I compare this to our witnessing. It is impossible, based on my incomplete knowledge and my lack of pure motivation, for me to offer God one gift that is totally pure and unfettered by sin. But the wonderful news is that when I witness in Jesus' name—my incomplete offering to God—Jesus Christ, who took up the slack by providing righteousness to my unrighteous life, will likewise take up the slack and provide pure motivation as He receives and blesses my gift.

Mary presented her gift to the living. Jesus accepted it as one dying, and thereby purified the motivation.

Just as Jesus received Mary's incomplete gift as total and pure, so He will receive the incomplete and impure offering of your efforts to witness in His name, and will bring them to perfection and total purity.

Don't be Afraid of the Consequences

You can win souls. However, there are many retardants to soul-winning that could hold you back. Satan loves to throw the consequences of what might happen into your mind and cause you to be afraid, hesitant, to make excuses.

In Ecclesiastes 11:4, there is an unusual verse: "He that observeth the wind shall not sow; and he that regardeth the clouds shall not reap." If you are afraid that the wind may come later and blow away the seeds you have sown, you will never sow. If you are afraid the clouds will bring the rains during the harvest, you will never reap.

You must sow when it is time to sow and leave the winds to God. You must reap when it is time to reap and leave the rains to Him. All the consequences are in His hands, not yours. Never fear the consequences.

If you are afraid you will be embarrassed, this may be evidence that you have not died to self, and have not let Christ occupy the throne of your life. Carnal Christians are afraid they will be embarrassed if they witness for Jesus Christ. But Spirit-filled people, who have Christ upon the throne of their lives, can be free of fear of embarrassment. When they are rebuked while witnessing, they know that the non-Christian is actually rebuking Christ. If they are chastised, they know that the scoffers are chastising Him. For He is going through everything His people are going through. He is experiencing everything they are experiencing. And He knows exactly how to suffer chastisement because He did it before.

Remember? They sat Him down, and each one struck Him a blow. They struck His cheeks and said, "Prophet, who strikes Your cheeks?" They drove nails into His hands, into His feet. A thorn crown was rammed upon His head. A spear was pushed into His side. They derided Him, cursed Him, abused Him, yet He opened not His mouth. This all happened to Jesus to bring into being the Gospel to which we are witnesses.

The Vanity of Life

Because people are frustrated, they are eager to hear. They are infinitely more eager to find an answer than we can ever believe. Remember to whom you are going: the frustrated and unhappy, people who are searching for ways to get through life.

The Book of Ecclesiastes is a classic analysis of what the ungodly man goes through. And the basic theme of the book is disillusionment. Solomon, the writer of Ecclesiastes, tried absolutely everything: the acquisition of wisdom (1:12-18); worldly pleasure (2:1-3); art and agriculture (2:4-6); wealth (2:7-11); epicurism (eat, drink, and be merry) (2:24-26); observing all the social evils about him (4:1-16); religious duty (5:1-7); enjoyment of long life (6:3-12); evil women (7:25-28); and civil duties (8:1-5).

When it was all over, Solomon came to the conclusion that all of these pursuits were nothing but steps toward the grave. At the end of the book, he wrote of the purpose of life: "Fear God and keep His commandments: for this is the whole duty of man. For God will bring every work into judgment, with every secret thing, whether it be good, or whether it be evil" (12:13-14).

The whole purpose of life is to remember God and to keep His commandments, because He is going to someday bring everyone's works and secrets to light.

As you go out to witness, you will be talking to

people who are experiencing some of the things Solomon did. And such people know, deep down in their subconscious, that all is vanity (12:8).

"'The first of all the commandments is, "Hear, O Israel; the Lord our God is one Lord; And thou shalt love the Lord thy God with all thy heart, and with all thy soul, and with all thy mind, and with all thy strength; this is the first commandment'" (Mark 12:29-30). How will you love God? By doing what He says. The first act of love for God is to love His Son. If you don't love His Son, you do not rightly love God. When you lead a person to Christ, you need to remember that though he is in one of the stages of vanity, he can find fulfillment in Christ. And you have the answer to give to him. Doesn't that challenge you to want to go out this very hour and talk to someone about Jesus Christ?

Practice, Practice, Practice

I have learned much about soul-winning from people inside the church, but that has not been my only source. It is my policy that 50 percent of my close friends will be unsaved people. I listen as much to the world as I listen to the church and am constantly appalled at the fact that they do not speak the same language. They are more foreign to each other than Americans to Japanese. I have learned much from people outside the church—and to my friends who truly know the working of the secular mind, I owe so much.

Every book I ever read on soul-winning was written from the view of churchmen to the world. I am attempting to combine the best of communication and understanding that the best of these have to offer. There is a golden touch of soul-

Don't Be Afraid / 67

winning brought about by the presence of the Holy Spirit in the dedicated believer's life, but every craft is sharpened by study and practice. And there isn't a man, woman, or child who cannot be a better witness for Christ than he is now.

I assure you that if you will take the principles of this book to your heart and practice, practice, practice them, you will increase your soul-winning efficiency by 200 percent. If this claim is true, every dedicated Christian on earth owes it to himself and his Lord not only to study this book, but to see to it that all of his close friends get to study it.

Perhaps it would be a good plan to start a home Bible study on formulas that work. The series could be based on this book, and could be taught by a pastor or a layman. If you are a layperson, perhaps you could buy a copy of it for your pastor, urge him to read it, and ask him to allow you to teach a course in it. Or, ask him to teach it.

If 100 people in every church in America would take the principles of this book and put them into practice, it would be amazing how many souls could be won. Let us not say 100, let us say 10 in each church. Now, let us use the Southern Baptist Convention as an example to show how it could work.

I hold in my hand my little Cassio calculator. There are 35,000 Southern Baptist churches. Only 10 soul-winners in each one would total 350,000. If each soul-winner won one person per month this would result in 4,200,000 conversions per year.

But wait a minute. There are more than 350,000 Protestant churches in the United States. If 10 soul-winners could be trained in each of them and each soul-winner won only one person per month, the result would be 42 million conversions to Jesus Christ in just one year. The whole world could be won to Jesus Christ if only 10 Christians in each church in the world took personal soul-winning seriously and practiced it only three hours per week. The whole world could be won, based on those three hours per week. Think of the excitement of such a concept.

In fact, based upon 70 million people in the United States who claim to be born again, if during the next year each of the 70 million won only three people to Jesus Christ, every man, woman, and child in the United States could be saved. America is only one year away from total conversion. The only requirement is that Christians find the right formula and apply it every day somewhere.

The problem with the world is not that the devil has control of it or that God does not have a plan. The problem of the world is Christians who won't do what God told them to do. Ninety nine percent of all Christians live in carnal disobedience to Jesus Christ. If they will not do the primary priority activity laid down by Jesus, they are carnal, backslidden, cold, and living in a state of poor relationship with God the Father. Jesus said. "Go ye therefore, and teach all nations, baptizing them in the name of the Father, and of the Son, and of the Holy Ghost; teaching them to observe all things whatsoever I have commanded you. And, lo, I am with you alway, even unto the end of the world" (Matthew 28:19-20).

The very first thing Jesus said, is, "Go." The second thing He said is, "Baptize." The third thing He said is, "Teach." That means training disciples. The fourth thing He said is, "Observe all things whatsoever I have commanded you."

He promised that if you will do these four simple things, He will be with you to the end of the age. He

Don't Be Afraid / 69

did not promise to be with you to the end of the age if you do not do those four things. So why don't you eliminate everything else you are doing and just do those four things? You can change your world!

There is not a man, woman, or child in this country, in your church, or in your home who cannot understand these four concepts—"Go," "Baptize," "Teach," and "Observe." So why not set those as your family priorities, and your church priorities? Then "Draw back and have a revolution!"

EIGHT
Reverse Psychology and Auto-Suggestion

Reverse psychology is the method of taking the opposite view from what you really stand for. In witnessing one should be very careful in the use of this method, because the timing must be absolutely perfect, and only God can indicate the perfection of the timing.

One of the world's best teachers of motion picture acting is Jimmy Best. Jimmy teaches a very select group of uniquely talented young actors the nuances of the art. To put it mildly, he is not known for his piety nor is he famous for his anti-piety. He is a well-insulated, thoroughly liberated, modern American semi-hedonist. But yet he is a delicate and sensitive man. I first met him on the set of *Gator*. We sat in a mobile unit and talked for several hours. He was moderately open to me, very friendly, and an easy guy to like. I was quite certain as I studied the nuances of our relationship that any mention of God, Christ, church, or the Bible would literally turn him inside out. I met him on one or two occasions after that and we have become good friends.

Reverse Psychology and Auto-Suggestion / 71

Mr. Best has a special technique. At the end of his class, he selects 8 or 10 scenes from films or the theater and asks 15 or 20 young people to present these five-minute vignettes in a kind of showcase. Talent scouts, actors, casting directors, and agents are invited to this highly charged experience. Several stars have been discovered this way. At the close of the showcases, I was congratulating Jimmy on the way he had developed the talent of the young people.

He said, "You know, I'd kind of like for us to get together sometime." He meant it, but there was an element of reserve in his invitation. I knew what that reserve was—he was afraid I would corner him on "religion." And I knew that this was a good time for reverse psychology, so I said, "Jimmy, I'd like that very much; let's do get together, but only on one condition."

He asked, apprehensively, "And what is that?"

"That you don't push your religion on me." That sealed it and we did get together. The opportunity to witness to Jimmy came later.

I remember a very secular man in Palm Beach who liked me but was mortally afraid that I would pin him down on religion. I couldn't get an invitation from him—which is always better than inviting your prospect to be with you. So finally I invited him to come to me. He wouldn't. He liked me, but was afraid. One day I decided it was time for reverse psychology, so I called him.

"Jeff," I said, "I'm so tired of church I don't know what to do. I've been attending services all year, going to deacons' meetings, finance committee meetings, church business meetings, staff meetings ... and I'm burned out on church. I really need to get away. Why don't you pull your boat out of the dock and let's get out of here for a day. And I'll come if you'll invite me on one condition: that we won't talk about church."

He invited me. We didn't talk about church once, but we began building a good relationship. It opened the door for me to be able to witness to him sometime later.

Auto-Suggestion
While the title of this section may sound secular or psychological, I must affirm that the power of auto-suggestion is an instrument God can use to a tremendous degree. If you have studied the Scripture for many years, your mind is a veritable computer filled with information that needs to be correlated and aimed in a compact fashion toward the ultimate answer. This is where auto-suggestion comes in.

There would be someone I wanted to win to the Lord, but I didn't quite know how to go about it. The tested and true techniques did not work, so I would pray, "Lord, I want You to instruct my subconscious to be used by Your Holy Spirit to correlate all the facts. I truly want to win this person, but my conscious mind can't arrive at the correct method. Please help me." I'd go to bed with that prayer in mind.

It has happened several times that God the Holy Spirit works with my spirit, bearing witness with my subconscious. I wake the next morning not even thinking about the person, but later that day, all of a sudden, an answer comes clearly to mind.

Let me illustrate how it works. There was a man in my city, Jim, who seemed almost impossible to reach for Christ. He claimed to have been a Christian

Reverse Psychology and Auto-Suggestion / 73

in his earlier days, but either he was a terribly backslidden Christian or he had never been saved in the first place. He was a hard, bitter man, but one with tremendous potential because of his influential position. While I did everything I could to reach him, I couldn't find a handle. He had all his defenses up, all the time. In a situation like this, it is appropriate to relax the witness and build a relationship of pre-evangelism. This is what I did.

One evening I was disturbed and worried about Jim. He was greatly on my heart. I prayed and asked the Holy Spirit to instruct my subconscious. I was tired and wanted to go to bed and forget the whole thing. "Lord, please work it out and let me know in the morning what I ought to do."

The next morning while I was brushing my teeth, the thought came to mind: "Stop trying to win him and try to win his wife. Enlist him in the effort to win his wife."

He loved Edith very much. She was not a Christian and did not know how to become one; but she had never shown great resistance to the Gospel. I called Jim and said, "I want to enlist your help. This morning the Lord laid Edith on my heart and I want to win her to Jesus Christ and help her to find eternal life and happiness. She's such a dear person and she needs Christ. Don't you agree?" To my surprise, he readily agreed.

I went to their large, luxurious home. No sooner had we met and sat down in his study to talk than he excused himself. I turned to Edith, "This morning the Lord laid you on my heart, and I want to talk to you about Jesus Christ and tell you how much happiness He can bring you."

Tears started running down her cheeks. She was

very ready to come to the Lord. She opened her heart and received the Saviour.

Then I said, "Are you going to tell Jim, or shall I?"

She said, "I'll tell him." She called out to him, and he came back into the room. She said, "Jim, the most wonderful thing in the world has just happened to me. I received Jesus into my heart. I'm a Christian."

Tears came to Jim's eyes. He said, "Darling, I'm so happy for you."

I said, "Edith, next Sunday morning when I extend the invitation at the close of the sermon, I want you to come forward and publicly acknowledge that you have received Jesus Christ as your Saviour." She said she would be happy to.

On Sunday morning when she came down the aisle, I prayed that Jim would come with her, but he didn't. I baptized Edith that evening, with Jim sitting in the audience watching.

About a week later I was having lunch with them. I did not mention God, Christ, the Bible—anything religious. As we were eating, Jim said, "I'm mad at you."

I asked, "What have I done?"

He said, "Why did you let my wife receive Christ and be baptized into your church and not ask me to do the same thing? I want to make it right too. I want to be baptized. I can't have a wife who is a Christian and a member of the church, when her husband is not." So Jim became a Christian. The next Sunday morning he came forward in church and in the evening he was baptized.

This is a clear case of how the Holy Spirit works in the subconscious to help you. As you prepare to win someone to Christ, take two or three days to think and pray about it and instruct your subconscious to listen to the Holy Spirit's instructions. He who prays with groanings you cannot understand, and understands what is garbled for you, sometimes can't get through to your conscious self. But He can talk ever so gently and accurately to your subconscious. And He truly will do it.

NINE
People Who Find Fault With God

In Los Angeles I regularly appear on one of the most widely listened-to radio programs, "Religion on the Line." A perky, vivacious, glib, and loving woman, Carol Hemingway, is the hostess. A Catholic priest, a Jewish rabbi, and I are fed to the city of Los Angeles on these Sunday evenings.

The TV telephone is available to a listening audience potential of eight million. People call in, say all kinds of things, and raise all sorts of questions. They often seem to concentrate on me because of my belief in the absolute uniqueness of Jesus Christ. And for some pseudointellectuals, trying to make the born again person feel insignificant and unimportant is a joyous pursuit.

"God Is Unjust"

Again and again I hear people say that God is unjust. "If He created man, and then condemned him, there is no justice in God." In attempting to answer this, I have learned that the stumbling opinions of a minister will not suffice. I have to rely totally upon

People Who Find Fault With God / 77

spiritual weapons, not on carnal ones. The Sword of the Spirit does the job much better than I.

I reply something like this: God Almighty had a purpose when He created every human being. "Even everyone that is called by My name: for I have created him for My glory. I have formed him; yea, I have made him" (Isaiah 43:7). It's very clear that God did not create man in order to damn him, but on the contrary, that he might have a happy life of praise, and of glory and blessing from God. Everlasting joy and bliss should characterize the creative purposes of God for every man.

The second thing I tell them is that all of God's dealings with man point to His desire that every man should be saved and not lost. I often quote Ezekiel 33:11, "Say unto them, 'As I live,' saith the Lord God, 'I have no pleasure in the death of the wicked; but that the wicked turn from his way and live; turn ye, turn ye from your evil ways; for why will ye die, O house of Israel?'" That certainly declares that God cares for man and has good intentions for him. It doesn't appear that God wants to damn men; rather He wants to save them. The price God paid and the sufferings He endured to save man from eternal despair indicate that God realizes the wickedness of sin and has paid an awful price to justify man.

I then tell them that God never intends that man should be lost. If a man is eternally lost, it is because he has willfully rejected God's marvelous plan in Christ. God doesn't decide that man will be lost.

If a man deliberately stumbles over the crucified body of Jesus Christ, placed right in the gate of hell to keep him out of the place of torment, then it is man's fault. God created man to rejoice over God, but man has chosen another way. This is man's fault.

The justification of God is very greatly needed. Rebellious, sinful man constantly attempts to transfer his guilt to God, to God's people, and to God's work. The guilt needs to be transferred back where it belongs.

"God Has Not Made Himself Known"

Another call that often comes in on "Religion on the Line" states that God has not clearly revealed Himself to man. How can man know God if God isn't clear in the revelation of Himself? How can a father punish a child for not doing what the father wants him to do, if the father has not clearly revealed what he wants done?

Let it be clear that God never asks His children to do impossible things. God only asks them to do that which they can do. God says that people can know Him—know who He is, what He is like, and His divine purpose for man. Man says he can't know these things.

To the Romans, Paul wrote: "For the wrath of God is revealed from heaven against all ungodliness and unrighteousness of men, who hold the truth in unrighteousness; because that which may be known of God is manifest in them; for God hath showed it unto them. For the invisible things of Him from the creation of the world are clearly seen, being understood by the things that are made, even His eternal power and Godhead; so that they are without excuse" (Romans 1:18-20).

God has revealed Himself clearly, but man chooses not to see. God has spoken clearly, but man chooses not to hear. When God speaks clearly through His creation, through His Word, and through His children, and man deliberately rejects all of the light God turns on, then man is to blame and not God. Some people want Him to reveal Himself in ways other than those He has chosen. This becomes their problem, not God's.

"Christ Can't Be the Only Way of Salvation"

I was being hassled by several of the callers concerning my belief that Christ is the only Redeemer. My rabbi friend mildly chided me concerning my belief in the uniqueness of Christ as the way to heaven. And I asked him, "Rabbi, explain clearly how I or any other human being may go to heaven. Give your plan of salvation. Tell us about eternal life." He stuttered and stammered and could not give an explanation. Callers who denied the single uniqueness of Christ could not offer a plan of salvation. I came to the conclusion that the world has nothing to offer as an alternative to Christ. God has not stuttered. He has spoken very clearly so all men can hear that in Jesus Christ is the fullness of the Godhead bodily.

God has truly revealed Himself to man in Christ. "No man hath seen God at any time; the only begotten Son, which is in the bosom of the Father, He hath declared Him" (John 1:18). Then why is man ignorant of God? Why does man not want to find God? Sin and disobedience is the answer. Man has sinned; man is disobedient: "Because that, when they knew God, they glorified Him not as God, neither were thankful; but became vain in their imaginations, and their foolish heart was darkened" (Romans 1:21). Those who will not come by the way of the cross have darkened minds, darkened emotions, and darkened imaginations. They cannot come up with a clear statement as to how man can be saved.

I have been told that I am intolerant and bigoted

because I believe there is but one way to heaven. I asked my rabbi friend, as tactfully as I knew how, if I could join his temple, and yet believe in Jesus Christ as my personal Saviour.

He answered, "No." Then I said, "Rabbi, you're as narrow as I am. We're just narrow in different directions."

"Jesus Is Not the Son of God"

Some people say, "The reason I will not come to Christ is that I do not believe that He is God's son in any other sense than Buddha, Muhammad or Socrates are. I truly believe Jesus was an excellent man. I believe He was God's son only in the sense that even Ghandi was God's son."

In the New Testament, there is a Greek word *monogenes* (only begotten) which is used only five times, and always by the Apostle John. With this word John expressed the relationship of the Father to the Son. While the meanings of the word vary slightly in the different contexts, they show that:

- the Son of God was the sole representative of the being and character of God
- that God the Father and God the Son are eternally one
- that Christ possesses every attribute of pure Godhood
- that God fully revealed His character through the incarnation of the Son who was given as an object of faith
- that Jesus did not become the Son of God by His birth. The One who came as a baby in Bethlehem is eternally God.

God the Son is *omnipotent;* He can do all things. "Jesus came and spake unto them, saying, 'All power

People Who Find Fault With God / 81

is given unto Me in heaven and in earth'" (Matthew 28:18).

He is *omniscient;* He knows all things. "And immediately when Jesus perceived in His spirit that they so reasoned within themselves, He said unto them, 'Why reason ye these things in your hearts?'" (Mark 2:8)

He is *omnipresent.* He is everywhere. "Where two or three are gathered together in My name, there am I in the midst of them" (Matthew 18:20).

He is *eternal.* "In the beginning was the Word; the Word was with God, and the Word was God" (John 1:1).

He is the *Creator.* "In the beginning was the Word. . . All things were made by Him and without Him was not anything made that was made" (John 1:1, 3). "For by Him were all things created, that are in heaven, and that are in earth, visible and invisible, whether they be thrones, or dominions, or principalities, or powers; all things were created by Him and for Him" (Colossians 1:16).

He is King and should be worshiped: "And as they went to tell His disciples, behold, Jesus met them and said, 'All hail.' And they came and held Him by the feet and worshipped him. . . . Then they that were in the ship came and worshiped Him, saying, 'Of a truth thou art the Son of God'" (Matthew 28:9; 14:33).

"The Bible Is Full of Contradictions"

Some say, "How can you believe the Bible? It is so full of contradictions." When a student once said this to me, I acted surprised, "Oh, really are there a lot of them in the Bible?" I acted naive.

He said, "Yes, there are many of them."

I said, "If that's true, will you tell me one?"
He was silent.

I said, "Surely you have made an exhaustive study of the Bible and can come up with at least one since you said there are *many*." He continued to stammer.

B.H. Carroll said that of 1,000 difficulties in the Bible, he found 994 had been totally answered by archaeology or a proper translation of the Scriptures. The other 6, he said, will vanish just as the first 994 did, when he gets more information.

Thank God for the Bible. You can depend on it.

"The Bible Is Impure"

Some have charged that the Bible is impure. It is strange how one can make such a charge against a book that has inspired such purity of life. The best and purest characters in the world are constant readers of God's Word.

It is a lie to say the Bible is impure, but a person who says it must be dealt with. We can tell him that he is not telling the truth, but that won't win him. He is in need of straight talk.

You can refer him to Psalm 12:6 and 119:140, "The words of the Lord are pure words; as silver tried in a furnace of earth purified seven times. . . . Thy Word is very pure; therefore thy servant loveth it."

The impurity lies not in the Bible but in the sinner's own wicked heart: "Unto the pure all things are pure; but unto them that are defiled and unbelieving, is nothing pure; but even their mind and conscience is defiled" (Titus 1:15).

When the Bible gives an honest account of a man's sinful deed—as with David's sin with Bathsheba—the sinner reported in the story is punished and his repentance is clearly recorded.

David sinned and the Bible quotes David as saying,

> Wash me thoroughly from mine iniquity, and cleanse me from my sin. For I acknowledge my transgressions; and my sin is ever before me. Against Thee, Thee only, have I sinned, and done this evil in Thy sight; that Thou mightest be justified when Thou speakest, and be clear when Thou judgest. Behold, I was shapen in iniquity, and in sin did my mother conceive me. Behold, Thou desirest truth in the inward parts; and in the hidden part Thou shalt make me to know wisdom (Psalm 51:2-6).

"The Bible Is Not Inspired"

I knew a poet from my college days who had traveled around the world. After his travels he came to see me and we debated the Scriptures for two days. He said he had studied the Scriptures carefully and believed the Bible to be no more inspired than the writings of Wordsworth, Keats, or Shelley. "It is a book, a good book to be sure, but it is a book written by human hands. It is among the best literature in the world, but it has no deity in the writing, no participation of God. It is merely the best thinking of good men."

We turned to 1 Thessalonians 2:13, "For this cause also thank we God without ceasing, because, when you received the Word of God which you heard of us, you received it not as the word of men, but as it is in truth, the Word of God, which effectually worketh also in you that believe." This is a clear statement that the Bible is not the word of man, but the Word of God.

I said to my friend, "You must never, never forget

that you are fighting the Word of God. Don't be melodramatic or poetic about it; but be blunt and hard and realistic and honest about it. I'm laying every card on the table right in front of you as clearly as I know how."

Then we looked at 2 Peter 1:20-21, "Knowing this first, that no prophecy of the Scripture is of any private interpretation. For the prophecy came not in old times by the will of man; but holy men of God spake as they were moved by the Holy Ghost." This shows that the Bible was written by the Holy Spirit through men.

And 2 Timothy 3:16, "All Scripture is given by inspiration of God...." Again I told my friend that he was in contradiction with Scripture.

I didn't see him for a long time after our discussion. But many years later I saw him in church. He was vibrant in Jesus Christ. He said, "One of the turning points in my life was when you pointed out that I was fighting against the Word of God. I realized that you loved me and you were telling me the truth about myself."

"There Are Hypocrites in the Church"

A student once said to me, "I'm having real problems because there are too many hypocrites in the church."

I said, "Of course there are; there always have been and there always will be. Did you ever see a counterfeit $20.00 bill?"

"No, but I've heard of one," she said.

"Did you ever see a counterfeit $50.00 bill?"

She said, "I saw a picture in the paper of a bundle of counterfeit $50.00 bills."

I said, "Did you ever see a counterfeit nickle?"

People Who Find Fault With God / 85

She said, "No. A nickle wouldn't be worth counterfeiting."

"That's right. You say there are hypocrites in the church, but have you ever seen a counterfeit sinner, a counterfeit drunk, a counterfeit of anything that was worthless?"

"No."

"The reason you see counterfeit Christians is that the real Christian is worth counterfeiting. The fact that there are hypocrites in the church indicates that they are attempting in a worldly, secular, sinful way to imitate something very good. By saying that there are hypocrites in the church, you are paying the church a very high compliment."

I asked her if there were hypocrites in a lodge, a civic club, in the university.

She said, "Yes, of course."

I said, "Then why don't you quit college? You quit the church because there are hypocrites there, but you won't quit college and there are hypocritical students. You are inconsistent. You are judging the church by the worst Christians we have in it. Why don't you judge the church by the best Christians we have in it?"

Then I reminded her that no one has the right to judge anyone else, that God will hold him responsible for doing it. "Who art thou that judgest another man's servant? To his own master he standeth or falleth. Yea, he shall be holden up; for God is able to make him stand. . . . But why dost thou judge thy brother? Or why dost thou set at naught thy brother? For we shall all stand before the judgment seat of Christ" (Romans 14:4, 10).

She realized she was judging the people in the church. I continued, "God will hold you responsible for your own sins, for your own inconsistencies, not for the sins and inconsistencies of other people. Since you know how Christians ought to live, don't you think God will hold you responsible for living that way? As it says in Luke 12:47-48, 'And that servant, which knew his Lord's will, and prepared not himself, neither did according to His will, shall be beaten with many stripes. But he that knew not, and did commit things worthy of stripes, shall be beaten with few stripes.'"

"All Will Ultimately Be Saved"

One woman once asked, "Don't you believe that all people ultimately will be saved? Or are you one of those narrow-minded bigots who believe that people will be lost, in spite of the fact that they live good, clean lives?"

My reply was, "I hope I'm not a bigot. I *am* biblical, and the Bible says that men who have not received Jesus Christ as their personal Saviour are lost."

She asked, "Just where does it say that in the Bible?"

"In 1 Corinthians 15:22: 'For as in Adam all die, even so in Christ shall all be made alive.' This verse clearly states that men must receive eternal life and that men are made alive in Christ. It says the whole race of mankind died, physically, spiritually, psychically, and emotionally in Adam; and the whole race rises physically, spiritually, psychically, and emotionally in Christ."

I also referred her to 1 Timothy 2:3-4: "For this is good and acceptable in the sight of God our Saviour; who will have all men to be saved, and to come to the knowledge of the truth."

Scripture indicates that man has some part to play in his salvation. Luke 13:3 says that man must repent. John 3:36 tells us that he must believe. Proverbs 28:13 says he must forsake his sins. And John 5:40 says he must come to Christ.

These are things people must do if they are to be saved. They cannot be saved if they do not believe on the Lord Jesus Christ. This isn't bigotry; it's biblical theology.

I referred the woman to Matthew 25:41-46,

Then shall He say also to them on the left hand, "Depart from Me, ye cursed, into everlasting fire, prepared for the devil and his angels. For I was an hungered, and you gave Me no meat; I was thirsty, and you gave Me no drink; I was a stranger, and you took Me not in; naked and you clothed Me not; sick, and in prison, and you visited Me not." Then shall they also answer Him, saying, "Lord, when saw we Thee an hungered, or athirst, or a stranger, or naked, or sick, or in prison, and did not minister unto Thee?" Then shall He answer them, saying, "Verily, I say unto you, inasmuch as you did it not to one of the least of these, you did it not unto Me." And these shall go away into everlasting punishment; but the righteous into life eternal.

A person is not saved if he has not repented of his sins and believed on Christ. (See Revelation 20:15; 21:8; 2 Thessalonians 1:7-9).

"I'll Have to Give Up All My Fun"

So many people want to have their own way. The Book of Proverbs speaks about this.

- "There is a generation that are pure in their own

eyes, and yet is not washed from their filthiness" (30:12).

- "The way of a fool is right in his own eyes; but he that hearkeneth unto counsel is wise" 12:15).
- "There is a way that seemeth right unto a man, but the end thereof are the ways of death" (14:12).

Jesus said we are to enter in "at the straight gate; for wide is the gate, and broad is the way, that leadeth to destruction, and many there be which will go in thereat. Because straight is the gate and narrow is the way, which leadeth unto life, and few there be that find it" (Matthew 7:13-14).

And the Apostle Peter wrote, "For the time is come that judgment must begin at the house of God; and if it first begin at us, what shall the end be of them that obey not the Gospel of God? And if the righteous scarcely be saved, where shall the ungodly and the sinner appear?" (1 Peter 4:17-18)

Ecclesiastes 11:9 says, "Rejoice, O young man in thy youth, and let thy heart cheer thee in the days of thy youth, and walk in the ways of thine heart, and in the sight of thine eyes; but know thou, that for all these things God will bring thee unto judgment." You will be brought into judgment if you choose to go your own way and not God's way.

In 2 Peter 2:12 we read, "But these, as natural brute beasts, made to be taken and destroyed, speak evil of the things they understand not; and shall utterly perish in their own corruption."

And yet there is much in Scripture that shows the very positive aspects of becoming a Christian. I did not begin to live until I began to live for Jesus Christ. I did not know what sheer enjoyment was until I gave my life to Him. God has a plan of joy, and when you give yourself to Him, He can fulfill it in your life.

"People Are Reincarnated"

Once I and several others had the opportunity to dine with Richard Bach, the author of *Jonathan Livingston Seagull* and other popular books. Mr. Bach is a charming, urbane, bright young man. The conversation was most exhilarating. Someone asked Mr. Bach, "Do you believe in reincarnation?" Richard Bach replied, "Of course, I believe in reincarnation. I don't know of any intelligent person who doesn't."

I had enjoyed myself so much up to that point. I prayed that the Lord would give me a chance to speak concerning the subject. Just as I prayed, Mr. Bach looked at me and asked, "What do you think of reincarnation?"

I answered, "May I ask a question that was asked 1,600 years ago by St. Augustine, Bishop of Hippo, that has not been answered yet, at least to my satisfaction? If reincarnation is true and life reincarnates itself instantly, why doesn't the population remain the same?"

The subject was changed rapidly by a gracious hostess who wanted to get us all off the hook.

Young people all across the country are deluded by the idea of reincarnation. The Scriptures say that "it is appointed unto men *once* to die, but after this the judgment" (Hebrews 9:27). Not several times to die, but just once, and then judgment.

The rich man died and was buried. In hell he lifted up his eyes in torment.

Lazarus died and was in the bosom of Abraham.

Jesus said to the thief on the cross, "Today thou shalt be with Me in Paradise" (Luke 23:43).

Reincarnation would negate the atoning work of Jesus Christ. If a person lived several lives, he might be converted in one life and lost in the next. On which life would he be judged? There is not one word of Scripture which teaches or even infers reincarnation.

"My Friend Is Jewish"

It is difficult to lead a Jewish person to Christ, but it is becoming more and more possible to share your faith with him and find a ready response.

The greatest way to win him is to truly be his friend, to honestly love and care for him as a human being.

In witnessing to Jewish people refer them to Psalms 22 and 69, Isaiah 53, and Zechariah 12:10. Show them that Christ is literally the fulfillment of all the messianic prophecies of the Old Testament. They seem to find difficulty in understanding how the Messiah of the Jews could go through the humiliation and suffering which Christ endured in Gethsemane and on the tree. Tie in the image of the Sacrifical Lamb with the phrase used by John the Baptist who said, "Behold, the Lamb of God, which taketh away the sin of the world" (John 1:29).

A Christian who works in West Los Angeles said, "The young Jewish people are asking very embarrassing questions of their rabbis. They are demanding expiation for their sins, and the only thing the rabbis seem to be able to tell them is, "There is no such thing as guilt," or "Go see your psychiatrist."

Jesus did away with the Old Testament sacrificial system. Salvation is now found only in His shed blood. This is why His shed blood is so important. He was the Lamb to replace all lambs.

Christ is the one sin offering to take away the sin of the world. I always show Jews that fact, and tell

People Who Find Fault With God / 91

them of the severe punishment which is meted out if one rejects Jesus Christ as Saviour:

> For if we sin willfully after that we have received the knowledge of the truth, there remaineth no more sacrifice for sins, but a certain fearful looking for of judgment and fiery indignation which shall devour the adversaries. He that despised Moses' law died without mercy under two or three witnesses; of how much sorer punishment, suppose ye, shall he be thought worthy, who hath trodden under foot the Son of God, and hath counted the blood of the covenant, wherewith He was sanctified, an unholy thing, and hath done despite unto the Spirit of grace?" (Hebrews 10:26-29)

TEN
Witness During the Crises of Life

There's a church in Columbus, Ohio that centers its entire ministry around eight crises of life: birth, childhood, conversion, adolescence, marriage, economic stress, sickness, and death. These are ideal times to be a witness for Jesus Christ.

Birth

In counseling with expectant parents, it has been my job and pleasure to be able to show them the necessity of giving their child a Christian father and a Christian mother. Many times when a couple marries, they do not think of deep spiritual things, but put them off by saying, "We'll face those matters when our first child comes." I always keep that in mind and take them up on it by calling them when I hear that the mother is expecting a child. I have led expectant mothers to Jesus, young fathers in the waiting room while waiting for a child to be born, or a couple after the child is brought home.

Another opportunity is on the day the parents dedicate themselves to the rearing of the child. In the churches I have served, we have dedication services in which we emphasize to the parents that they should both be Christians and should both see that the child is brought up in a Christian home.

There are extremely sad times connected with childbirth that are vital times for sharing the Gospel of Christ. I once lead a father to Christ when his wife died in childbirth, and a mother and father to the Lord when their child was stillborn. A pastor must become soul-minded in the midst of crises. He needs to realize that it is often difficult to get parents' minds off the crisis and on to Christ, who can meet them in their time of sorrow.

Childhood

The happiest times in my life are when I can be with bright, young children, to help give them the kind of Christian nurture and pre-evangelism they need. So many children are from divided homes that it is incumbent upon the churches to give to the children as many father figures as possible.

I remember Ken Johnson, the only pitcher in the history of the major leagues to pitch a no-hitter and lose it. Ken was a member of my church. One day he came to me and said, "Doc, as you know, I'm retiring from baseball and I'd like to make myself available to work in the church anywhere you want me. I want to serve the Lord in the most necessary place."

At first I thought, "Well, he'll make a good Sunday School teacher for young men. A great pitcher like that would be a tremendous influence on young adults." I prayed about the matter and after thinking about it long and hard I said, "Ken, the First Baptist Church of West Palm Beach has many tiny children who are from broken homes. They don't have father figures and they need a strong, 6-foot, 4-inch, 220-pound man to sit down on the floor and tell them about Jesus and His love."

Ken did not hesitate one minute. He said, "Doc, if you feel that's where I can best serve, I'll take it." He became a worker in the children's department. You should have seen those little children swarming around him, holding their hands out to him, loving him. I've seen him walk out the door with a child hanging on each leg and each arm, and one around his neck. Ken has been happy and effective, serving as a Christian influence in the pre-evangelizing of little children.

Conversion

The conversion of children is an arena of great controversy. There are those who believe a person should not be converted until 12 or 13 years of age. They hold to the fact that Jesus was in the temple when He was 12. But this story was not intended to set a time when children can be converted.

We live in an age of precociousness. So much brightness is instilled into the minds of children, by television and advanced teaching methods, that the conversion age has actually gone down. Twenty years ago, the average age of conversion was nine years of age. I believe it is lower now, seven or eight, and sometimes a very bright child will see the difference between right and wrong and will give himself to Jesus Christ at five years of age.

I realize the dangers in this kind of emphasis. There are two things you should look for in the child: (a) an understanding of the difference between right and wrong, (b) a feeling that he is a sinner. This is shown by verbal expressions of a sense of guilt.

However, a consciousness of guilt should not be fostered by other people. Such a child may come to his parents in a natural way and say, "I don't feel good in my heart; I want Jesus as my Saviour," or "I am sorry that I haven't treated my sister right, and I want to give my life to Jesus." Children are very literal and think in terms of hard pragmatism. Most often they do not say, "I am a sinner." Rather "I'm sorry for the way I've treated Billy," or "I love daddy and mother and I want to love Jesus too." These may be expressions of guilt and expressions of a sense of need of conversion or completion in their lives. Parents should not belittle a child's request to accept Christ and to be baptized into the church. They should be wide open to these signals. Most pastors will be happy to help any parents who want to talk to their children about personal salvation. I have seen young children who truly converted to Jesus Christ go on to live spiritually fruitful lives for the Lord.

One time when D.L. Moody gave an invitation, a man over fifty and a child of nine came forward. D.L. Moody said, "Isn't that wonderful? A conversion and a half."

Someone said, "You mean the man is the conversion and the child is the half?"

D.L. Moody replied, "No, sir. The child is the conversion, the man is the half. The child has a whole life to live for God; the man has only half a life to live for Him." Childhood is a wonderful time to emphasize pre-evangelism, and then some very gentle but saving evangelism when the situation seems ripe.

Adolescence

Adolescence is a very critical time for every member of the family. More mistakes are made by adolescents—and by their parents in reaction to them—at this critical juncture in their lives than at any other time. It is such a delicate period that it demands spiritual sensitivity of the most advanced sort.

There is only one thing worse than adolescence and that is the absence of it when it is supposed to be happening. Delayed adolescence is the real culprit in most tragic situations. It is better for a young person to make all kinds of ridiculous remarks, hold all sorts of radical views while he is in his mid to late teens, than for him to run away with his secretary when he is 40. In my opinion, the chief cause of divorce in America today is delayed adolescence

The worst thing that can be said to an adolescent son is, "Be a man." He is not a man; he is an adolescent. And for one to try to make a man out of him, simply because he has become man-sized, is a terrible mistake. Parents can rest assured that it is a good thing if their son or daughter is having adolescence right on schedule. And they can be comforted by the fact that it will be over in a year or two.

Both of our children had very pronounced adolescent experiences. They fought the battle of drugs, rebellion, flight reaction from stress to the point that one of them ran away from home at 16. I had to fly to Washington to bring her back to Mother and home again. It was a great learning experience for all of us.

I remember when Martha turned 13 years of age. We did what probably would be considered an insane thing to do. I told Martha that puberty was a great time in her life, of rejoicing and celebrating God's great gift of life and creativity. I went to the bank and withdrew $500, and Martha and I flew to New York for a week. I took her to the Broadway show, "You're a Good Man, Charlie Brown," got her hair fixed by a New York stylist, bought her some long, white gloves, had her face made up, took her to the nicest restaurants in New York, introduced her to Jack Dempsey and Sebastian Cabot. We had a great time! Adolescence was born in Martha's life with a celebration.

Adolescence is not a curse that descends to be meted out by Satan. It is the birth of new life, and as all life has its labor pains, even so the birth of manhood or womanhood has its discomfort. The birthpangs are the hard part; the beautiful maturity is the good part.

I've led many adolescents to Jesus Christ. I've sat down on their front porches and helped them fix broken bikes and then led them to Jesus Christ. I taught one to ride a motorcycle and led him to Jesus Christ. I took another for a plane ride and led her to Jesus Christ. So many wonderful opportunities present themselves with adolescents. They will love you with an undying love and support you with powerful emotion. Some of them are the best Christians I know. They are fun to be with and exhausting to follow, but they always seem to come up with the brightest, most witty charm.

No one can love Jesus Christ as an adolescent can. A mid-teen boy or girl can pray as you've never heard anyone pray, and can witness without fear. I've seen them win hundreds of fellow teenagers to Jesus Christ. The people who devote their lives to teenagers make a vitally important contribution. I envy people who for 30 years have been winning teenagers to Jesus Christ. God keeps them eternally young; and they have so much fruit to look back upon and see it bearing spiritual fruit in the world through the lives of those they've won.

Since teenagers see everything in 3D-technicolor, a person who speaks to them must speak with brightness, vivaciousness, strength, and enthusiasm. When witnessing to them, be certain that you are very clear in your biblical interpretation. And remember, they take every word very seriously. What you say and what you are before them will preach as through a public address system to their personalities. So watch your words and your actions as you carry the news of Christ to them.

When I was 17 the world was hit by a terrible war. War is an awful time. God's plan is that the sons bury their fathers, not that the fathers bury their sons. I had some great high school friends—fellow athletes—who were beautiful young men: Robert Hammonds, Gene Clark, John Porshea, John Henry Chapman, and David Story. These were great guys. They went off to war, and that terrible war took their lives. It was through the crucible of the pain that I endured in the loss of my friends, through the crystal tears of my sorrow, that God called me to preach the Gospel of Jesus Christ. I was deeply moved and touched by their deaths, and felt that I had to somehow live the lives of my five friends.

I won't soon forget how delicately my pastor, Reverend Purcell, dealt with me in this time of loss. Very quietly and very tenderly, as I sat in his car weeping, he shared with me how much it meant to him to see me responding spiritually to God's call to the ministry.

There were those who said that I had responded to the call out of emotion, because of the loss of my friends. Thirty-five years later, I would say that God used the tenderness of my adolescent mind and heart, and the sorrow that was generated in the loss of my friends, to point out that which had been lurking in my soul in seed form for many years—that God was truly calling me to preach His Word. There have been many times when I've wanted to quit, but I could not respond to any siren call of any secular pursuit. My mind simply could not consider anything but preaching His Word in one form or another throughout this earth. Adolescence is a crucial time because so many lifetime decisions are made in those years.

Marriage

Marriage is a wonderful time to lead someone to Jesus Christ. I remember a young groom, handsome to a fault, dressed in a magnificent gray tux, waiting with me in the side room while the parents were being seated and the soloist was singing. He said something like this: "Dr. Moody, I'm going out there to marry one of the nicest Christian girls in the world. To me she's the best human being on earth, as near to Jesus as anyone could be. Dr. Moody, she asked me a question last week, and I haven't been able to get it out of my mind. She said, 'Ronny, are you a Christian?' I told her I was. But, Dr. Moody, it isn't true. I thought being a Christian was being an American because, after all, isn't this a Christian nation? But last Sunday as I sat in church I heard you preach, your message touched my mind and my heart. And I realized that conversion is an experience we have and not a gift that comes along with being born in this free country."

And then the bridegroom said, "But I don't understand how one is saved."

So I opened the Bible from which I was to perform the ceremony, and led him to understand that all men are sinners, and must be saved. He bowed his head and accepted Jesus as his personal Saviour. He was one the nicest young men I've ever know.

During the wedding ceremony he whispered to his bride that he had a wedding gift for her. When they knelt to pray, he whispered to her, "My wedding gift to you is that Dr. Moody led me to Jesus while we were waiting to come out for this ceremony." She began to weep, and when they stood and he kissed her, tears were rolling down her cheeks. I have never known a happier bride in my entire ministry.

Weddings are a wonderful time to lead people to Christ. Parents of the bride and groom are very open at that time, and brothers and sisters also. Pastors may be able to lead the bride or groom to Jesus Christ during marriage counseling. A good witnessing pastor will not assume that people are Christians, and will see a wedding as an opportunity to share the faith with the young couple and others in the wedding.

Economic Stress

When a man is down economically, he is up spiritually. Remembering this see-saw will help you to time your witness most effectively.

Our church has a ministry of economics in which we operate an employment agency. Our director, Sandy Quinn, counsels people concerning job opportunities, training, and writing resumes. She averages finding positions for 40 people per month. These range from minimum wage jobs to top executive positions. Nothing else we do brings more unsaved people into our church. It also serves as a ministry to those already in Christ and in the church fellowship. Recently a young banker had lost his position and was quite discouraged. I told him to see Sandy. The next day she steered him to a position with a bank in Los Angeles. He and his wife are now both very active in our church family.

Helping someone in economic stress is a visible, tangible way the church can bear witness of Christ. James 2:15-18 speaks to this issue:

> "If a brother or sister be naked and destitute of daily food, and one of you say unto them, 'Depart in peace, be ye warmed and filled;' notwithstanding ye give them not those things which are needful to the body; what doth it profit? Even so faith, if it hath not works, is dead, being alone. Yea, a man may say, 'Thou hast faith and I have works;' Shew me thy faith without thy works and I will shew thee my faith by my works."

This is evangelical Christianity's most glaring weakness. Many people seem strong in the faith but will not so much as raise a hand to feed and clothe a brother or sister. It is a major stumbling-block which has not gone unnoticed by the pagan world. Offer economic help, and your witness will instantly increase.

Sickness

It is obvious that this is prime-time witnessing, and the devil has an artful trick to block prime-time effectiveness. He puts into the mind of the would-be witness: "I must wait to witness to Mary: if I do it now, she will think I am referring to death. This will upset her too much."

I fell for that lie one time and sinned against the Spirit's prompting to share my faith. I visited an unsaved friend in the hospital but I would not share

Christ with her. My associate pastor, Dan Griffin, visited her later that evening, witnessed clearly and she received Christ into her life. I was guilty and he grew in grace!

Failure to use laypeople in hospital visitation is an area of stewardship profligacy in which the churches should repent. There are hundreds of laypeople who would love to learn gentle hospital witnessing.

I wouldn't exactly recommend the method used by Sam Jones, the evangelist of the late 1890s. Sam was visiting a man who had been told that he would never leave the hospital alive.

"Oh, Brother Jones, I know I'm an awful sinner. I've cursed your campaigns, the churches, and I've called Christianity a religion for old women and children. If God will get me out of here, I'll repent, come to the altar, be saved, join the church, and live a Christian life. Please pray that I'll get well."

Sam Jones knelt and called out in full voice: "God, if he means it, let him live. If he doesn't, KILL HIM!"

There is a better way. I have discovered that calm confidence on my part makes a lot of difference. An assured witness causes great response on the part of the physically ill. Use the methods outlined in this book. Beware of one cardinal sin of some personal evangelists in hospital visitation—don't promise them healing if they get right with God. Keep salvation and healing separate. Why?

Because of the "rice Christianity" principle. Many starving people have "received Christ" because the missionaries would feed them if they were in the church. Many who are ill receive Christ in order to be healed. This, of course, dilutes the Gospel and makes *healing*, not Christ, the object or purpose of faith. The result is a spurious salvation.

Death

I remember an old maxim for pastors about funeral sermons: "Don't preach them into heaven." Which means, if they have not received Christ, don't preach as though they have.

Perhaps another maxim for funerals should be, "Don't preach the families *out* of heaven." In other words, don't fail to preach the Gospel to the family. Here Satan puts another bit of sand into the machinery. He will say it to the pastor at every funeral. "Now, don't take advantage of their bereaved condition to share your faith."

A young neighbor of ours in West Palm Beach was killed in an automobile accident. He had scores of young friends. I decided to offer to talk to his many friends about what happened to Roger. They were invited to a neighbor's house. I never met with more fierce resistance, from man or demon.

- "What are you trying to do?"
- "You're taking advantage of the situation."
- "Roger would be embarrassed if he knew about this."
- "No one will come!"

I felt the Inner Voice tell me to do it, and I went ahead. More than 50 young men came. I felt that the resistance meant that God had a plan for the moment.

I spoke openly and plainly about Jesus Christ. God gave me a boldness I could not self-muster, and 24 young adults received Christ that day.

Another unique method is to invite a dozen unsaved friends to visit a dying Christian. Let the patient share the Gospel with these friends. God can use a dying Christian in a powerful, telling way.

You don't like this method?

Where did I get such a silly idea?
From God.
He used the dying witness of Stephen to a young man named Saul, who became Paul the Apostle.

What a way to go to heaven! Witnessing while dying.

If the patient is too weak to speak, a little note with a stack of tracts could be placed in the hospital room. The note could read, "Bob wants you to have one of these."

This is a highly effective use of tracts.

People will read them for Bob's sake and will repent for Jesus' sake.

In Chinese the word *crisis* means "veiled opportunity." Every crisis is a veiled opportunity to witness for Christ.

ELEVEN
Learn to Close

If you can't close, you are not a soul-winner; you're just a conversationalist. Every topflight soul-winner is a powerful closer, because he acts on the principle that what he says in the presentation of the Gospel is of the utmost importance and the ultimate answer to the deepest needs of the person to whom he talks.

The entire presentation is aimed toward finalizing the decision. Therefore, the most important soul-winning aspect is the closing. For, if you do not know how to draw a person to a decision and to close the transaction, all the presentations and techniques of evangelism in the world won't work.

The non-closer is the non-soul-winner.

What good does it do to act as though you are a soul-winner if you actually never win anyone! Some people hide behind hypercalvinism at this point. They say, "It is only my job to tell the story of Christ. The results are entirely up to God."

I question that, after 35 years in the ministry, I am convinced that God has done absolutely everything in communicating His truth to man—up to the point of infringing upon the will of the unsaved man. If you use a poor technique which stands in the way of a person making a decision, then your technique is in the way. Do not blame God for your poor methods.

When?

What is the best time to make the close? The answer is, "When the person you are witnessing to is ready." This is very difficult to tell at times. One person will seem to be agreeing with you on every point; but when you press the claim of Jesus Christ to him, he will use one excuse after another. Another person may not seem quite ready; but when you press the claims of Christ upon him, he is ready to receive.

I've never been able to be quite sure when a person is ready for the close. And since I'm not sure, I go ahead and give him the opportunity to receive Christ.

Once I visited a friend dying of cancer. He began using one excuse after another to not accept Christ. I said, "Frank, two hours ago the doctor walked in and told you you were dying of cancer. You are using the same excuses you used before you knew you were going to die. Frank, I love you so much. Throw away all those flimsy excuses and receive Jesus Christ as your Saviour right now."

He burst into tears, "I was using the old excuses, but I don't want to use them now. I'm only afraid that God will not want to receive me, because I've wasted so much time and refused Him so long. Now that I know I'm dying—what a pitiful way to be saved!"

I said, "Frank, there is no pitiful way to be saved. Every way is glorious. The thief on the cross didn't hesitate to say, 'Lord, remember me when Thou comest into Thy kingdom.' Jesus died so you could live. Why don't you live the rest of your days in service for Him?" He accepted Christ, lived three more months, and won over a dozen people to Jesus Christ from his sick bed. There is never a good time to close; there is never a bad time. Offer to pray with the person. He might need just that simple encouragement to make the decision he needs to make.

How?

A friend of John D. Rockefeller asked him, "John, you bought a million dollar life insurance policy from an upstart, didn't you?"

"Yes," said Mr. Rockefeller.

"John, I've played golf with you for nine years. You knew I was in the insurance business. Why didn't you buy the policy from me, your old friend?"

Rockefeller said, "You never asked me. He did."

At a supersalesmen's convention, the leading appliance salesman in the nation came forward to receive his award. He was very ordinary looking. People asked, "How had he done it? He is such a common looking person."

Telegrams and phone calls failed to elicit from him any profound secret for his success. He insisted it was just a matter of doing his job. One man was convinced that he was covering up some super secret, so he flew to the salesman's home town, had dinner with him, and asked for his great secret.

The salesman said, "There is nothing to it. There is no secret."

Exasperated, the other man said, "OK, there's no secret. But just tell me how you go about making a sale."

"That's easy," the salesman replied, "you know that 32-page booklet you sent to each of us telling the sales feature of your appliance? Well, when I sit down with a prospect I simply show him page 1 of the manual. When I get to the bottom of the page, I ask him to buy. If he doesn't, I read page 2 and ask him to buy again. And so on. I read as many of the 32 pages as are necessary until the man buys."

The wide-eyed sales manager recovered from his astonishment long enough to ask, facetiously, "And what if he doesn't buy after you finish reading page 32?"

The common man, the supersalesman, calmly replied, "I start all over again on page 1."

Here are several closing techniques you can use:

1. Don't let prospective Christians sidetrack you from the closing. People sometimes listen patiently to the Gospel. But when they sense that you are going to ask them to receive Christ, they start throwing up one story after another to try to move you in another direction. Don't let them do it!

2. Review the points of the Gospel and then lead right into the close. That sometimes causes them to realize the truth of the Gospel and makes them want to make a decision for Christ.

3. Imagine what it is going to be like when they have received Jesus as Saviour. Tell them how happy they're going to be, that they're going to have the problem of sin, sorrow, and death solved. And then, make the close.

4. Imagine for them what it will be like if they do not receive Christ as Saviour. They can go through this life as happy as an unsaved person can be, but then they're going to face the judgment and eternity. Don't hesitate to talk to sinners about hell. They know what it is, for they go through it every day.

5. Appeal to emotions. Emotions are a very vital

Learn to Close / 109

part of personality. More people have been won by tears than by arguments.

6. Watch for "willingness" signals. Sometimes a person will begin nodding his head to you. You must keep nodding your head to him and you will lead him right into receiving Christ.

7. Use the point-blank method. Stop talking and say, "John, I've come to the time when you should receive Jesus Christ. Do it right now. I'll lead you in a prayer, and you follow me." Very often they will.

8. Get a strong closing story, something that really touches the heart. Not necessarily a deathbed story, but a dramatic story of what happened when someone gave his life to Jesus.

9. Use "Yes, Mr. Wilson." "Yes, John."
"Yes, it is true that God's Word is infallible."
"Yes, it is true that Jesus died on the cross for you."
"Yes, it is true that we are all sinners."
"Yes, it is true that if you believe in Christ you will be saved."
"Yes, it is true that if we will confess with our mouth the Lord Jesus and believe in our hearts that God has raised Him from the dead we shall be saved."
"Yes, all these things are true."
"And now I will lead you in a prayer as you say yes to Jesus Christ. Let's pray together, and you pray after me."

10. The either-or method. Do not ask a question that can receive a yes-or-no answer. Ask the question based on either-or. "John you can receive Christ either by my leading you in a prayer or by our silently bowing our heads and your telling Jesus that you want to receive Him into your heart. Which way shall it be?" Very often he will just bow his head and

quietly give his life to Christ. When he finishes his silent prayer, look at him and say, "John, you did receive Jesus into your heart, didn't you. I can tell."

Also you may use either-or method with reference to his being baptized into the church fellowship. "The pastor can baptize you this Sunday evening or next Sunday evening. Which would be better for you?"

11. The "do-it-now" method. After making several efforts to lead the person to Christ, the person witnessing picks up his Bible and briefcase, cordially thanks John for his courtesy and time. He is assured that his visit has been welcome and pleasant, then the Christian says, "Yes, it has been a profitable visit. Before I go do you mind if I ask you one more question?"

"No, indeed," says John, who is relaxed now that the man is leaving.

"John, you know that I'll be coming back. I've driven nine miles to see you tonight. Why don't you just settle the issue with me right now while we are standing at the door. No one is here but the two of us. Would you like me to lead you in a prayer of acceptance of Christ, or would you like to pray silently? Let's bow our heads and settle it right now."

Don't be turned off by the use of techniques in witnessing. Remember the story of the lady who criticized D.L. Moody for his methods of winning people.

"I agree with you," Moody said, "I don't like the way I do it either. Tell me, how do you do it?"

The lady said, "I don't do it."

Moody replied, "Then I like my way of doing it better than your way of not doing it."

Learn to Close / 111

The point—do it!

"How shall we escape if we neglect so great salvation?" (Hebrews 2:3)

"Behold, *now*, is the accepted time; behold, *now* is the day of salvation" (2 Corinthians 6:2).

TWELVE
Perpetuate the Gospel

After I tried several unsuccessful follow-up ideas, I decided to read the directions. God has a general plan, but He leaves the specifying to us.

What is included in the general plan? Jesus said, "Go ye into all the world and preach the Gospel. . . . baptizing them in the name of the Father, and of the Son, and of the Holy Ghost; teaching them to observe all things whatsoever I have commanded you; and lo, I am with you alway, even unto the end of the world" (Mark 16:15; Matthew 28:19-20).

The Great Commission included the following:
- going
- going into all the world
- preaching to everyone
- baptizing them
- teaching them
- teaching to observe every teaching of Jesus
- practicing the presence of Jesus

A good follow-up program must include these elements. Let's briefly consider each one of them.

1. Going. The devil has won his battle for a

Perpetuate the Gospel / 113

believer's life if he can take the "go" out of him. The very first teaching to instill into a new believer is that going with the Gospel is a lifetime feature of the happy Christian life.

Many churches make the mistake of teaching a new Christian that he is to go, but they do not program church activities so that people do it.

The most successful evangelistic churches send their new converts out as observers with trained soul-winners. Often a new Christian can give the story of his newfound joy in a way that some older believers cannot.

I have found that the most effective witnessing ever done has been a new convert amateurishly sharing God's love story. The results both upon those witnessed to and the witness himself have been phenomenal.

During the Billy Graham campaign in Miami, it was my privilege to help Ernest Barber, a bank president, lead Jim Huband, a broadcast executive, to Jesus Christ. I was scheduled to speak to a large group of attorneys immediately after my conference with Barber and Huband. As soon as Jim accepted Christ, he said, "What is my next step?"

"Your next step is to come with me," I replied.

An hour later I was standing before these bright, attractive Miami lawyers. I told them that I knew they would be skeptical about the presentation of my case for Christianity unless I brought some evidence into the case. My premise was: "If Christ is real anywhere, He is real everywhere."

I presented my evidence, which was the witness of Jim Huband. Jim stood, spoke straight out for Christ, then pled with them all to surrender their lives to Him. And four of them did just that!

The point is that a new Christian is dying to tell the world about the fire of love in his heart. Don't tell him that he must go through a training session before he can be a witness. Get him going—fast!

In the Great Commission, Jesus literally said, "As you are going, be preaching My Gospel." Every incidental and seemingly accidental meeting is a small platform for a great Gospel. Jesus' encounters with the woman at the well, Zaccheus, and Nicodemus were all "chance" meetings that turned the informal or the incidental into the eternal.

The average American walks 115,000 miles during his lifetime. This is enougth to take him around the equator nearly five times. Every one of those steps should belong to Jesus Christ.

2. *Going into all the world.* I interpret this not only as a missionary motive but also as a motive of mission; not only as geographical but relational. My Lord is telling me to go everywhere in the world with the Good News, and also to take the Gospel into every world in which people find interest.

We are to go into the world of finance, music, art, science, literature, politics—and every other world with the message of salvation and hope. This opens up all of the creative potential of the mind of man spreading the good Lord's good Word.

The new convert can be led to relate his testimony to what he already knows. To that end, all of his history prepares him to tell the story of God's love.

An illustration of this is the small revival that has taken place in the professional athletic world, because a few athletes who found Christ went into their world to preach the Gospel to their team members.

If new Christian Bill is in the construction business, he should be shown right away how to share his faith

Perpetuate the Gospel / 115

with his fellow workers. The closer he is to conversion the greater his courage to witness.

Send up a big cheer for him when he witnesses. Don't make the mistake of saying, "I don't give him credit because only God should get the glory." Listen! There is a lot of difference between giving praise to God and giving appreciation to a saved sinner for witnessing. Thank your friend every time he tells someone about Jesus.

3. *Preaching to everyone.* That word *preaching* turns people off because of the churchy image of the clergyman in black suit, wing-tipped shoes, and serious countenance. It does no violence to the Scriptures to use the words "sharing," "witnessing," or whatever causes you to go tell someone about Jesus Christ.

Understand this one fact: God commands every born again human to give away his faith to everyone, everywhere. The drug pushers go to *everyone;* the liquor industry wants *everyone* to drink; the gambling combines want *everyone* to gamble. Why can't we Christians carry the Gospel to everyone? The only alternative to witnessing is to live in disobedient, sinful rebellion.

Help the new Christian to understand that *everyone* is his responsibility. A serious discipline in this direction is a must for every believer. Get the new person to walk directly from the altar to a course in *everyone-ism!*

4. *Baptizing them.* Many Christian leaders are deeply disobedient because they are thoroughly causal about baptism for the new believer. This is due to the shift in emphasis from local churches to transdenominational parachurch groups. Most of these are sound in the faith except that they do not

insist that all believers should be baptized into the local church fellowship.

There is no reference in the Scriptures to a person having accepted Christ and not being immediately baptized. Not once. Baptism is a clear teaching of our Lord, yet half of the Christian world is stuttering at this part of the Great Commission.

The new Christian is told by Jesus Himself to be baptized. No tradition or religious concept can supercede the weight of His demand. Every Christian leader should insist on this obedience by the new Christian.

5. *Teaching them.* The early church took the Great Commission to heart. They outlined the revolutionary command of Jesus into two parts; *heralding* the Gospel and *teaching* the believers. Heralding was called the *kerygma* and teaching was called the *didache.*

The *kerygma* was everyone's job, but the *didache* rested in the hands of the Apostles. This was termed "the Apostles' doctrine" (Acts 2:42). It is the church's job to see to it that every member be a witness. It is the pastor's responsibility to oversee the doctrinal teaching of the new Christian.

The church has the grandest opportunity to see that the warmth of the new Christian continues, in love for souls and love for the Word of God. Every fast-growing church has this double emphasis.

Churches do this work in many ways. My personal preference in overseeing the *didache* is to immediately enlist new Christians in a dynamic Sunday School class. This ties them into a pattern of studying Christian doctrine.

Many churches prefer new member classes and that is fine if it doesn't lead the new Christian away from Sunday School. To me, nothing makes a believer a continuing member of a church better than the Sunday School.

Chances are good that the new Christian is already a member of the Sunday School, because more converts come out of the Sunday School than from any other church activity, including the worship service. If that is not true in your church, perhaps you have a gold mine of potential that you never suspected.

The open secret of the church is that to win one person in one year outside the Sunday School, there must be 271 unsaved people signed up by a community church census. *To win one person in one year in Sunday School, there must be only three enrolled in a Sunday School class.* The key, therefore, is to spend most of your time enlisting new members for the Sunday School. This is even more productive than weekly personal soul-winning visitation. This is hard to believe, but it is true. It is six times more difficult to win a lost soul out in the community than it is to enroll him in a dynamic Bible study in Sunday School. My calculations of these figures tell me that Sunday School enrollment is twice as effective as house-to-house witnessing.

This does not mean that you do away with soul-winning programs. Do *both* and watch the church family grow.

6. *Teaching them to observe every teaching of Jesus.* There is a difference between *teaching* and *observing.* "Teaching them" is communicating facts to the new Christian. "Teaching them to observe" is teaching them to *act* upon the *fact.* It means investigating until one is gripped by the truth to the degree that he is moved to act upon the truth.

Learning without observing, hearing without doing—this is the great evangelical error of our day. The terrible tragedy of seeing masses thronging giant Bible-preaching churches, taking notes on thousands of legal pads, cracking Greek diphthongs and nibbling on Hebrew roots, with not enough resultant action to convert a chipmunk—this is a corruption that should evoke 96 theses on a 20th century Wittenburg Door!

Every new Christian should be taught judgment-bar honesty in studying the Word of God, in learning the practical principles from it, and then in applying them exactly as he thinks Jesus would do it.

I preached at the National Prayer Breakfast in Washington D.C. many years ago. I do not recall my entire message, but the closing was something like this:

> You want your world changed? Begin by reading the New Testament with Matthew 1:1 and continuing till you come to a clear, unmistakable command from Jesus Christ. Put your Bible down, go out and do what it says. Then come back and read till you come to another unmistakable teaching from God's Son. Again, put your Bible down and go out and confront society with your practical doing of what Christ says. Repeat this process again and again. By the time you reach Matthew 8, you will have changed the world.

I believe it!

If every new and old convert could demand this courage of himself, the results would change all mankind.

7. *Practicing the presence of Jesus.* If you are a Christian, you believe literally every syllable of the

Great Commission. The last phrase: "I am with you alway, even unto the end of the world (or age)," is the most important of all.

The new Christian must learn to not just believe this fact but to practice it. Practicing the presence of Jesus is the key to assurance, confidence in witnessing, and deep trust in prayer. A new believer who has these three factors active in his life can never be defeated or permanently discouraged.

Practicing the presence of Jesus is conditioned upon the other components of the Great Commission. The believer must be a going, heralding, baptized, teaching, observing believer. When this is true, Christ will always be involved in every event of his life.

The purpose of discipleship is to make witnesses of all Christians. No believer is discipled until he is evangelizing. Witnessing is not something you grow out of into "more mature" discipleship.

Witnessing is discipleship and discipleship is witnessing. Each dies without the other.